Sonhatsí:wa
Your True Self

Ganǫhkwásra' Family Assault Support Services

Writer/Editor
Stacy Tekonwanyahesen Hill

Illustrations by
Raymond R. Skye

Ganǫhkwásra' Publications

Copyright 2005 Ganǫhkwásra⁷ Publications

Any request for the reproduction of this book in whole or in part, must be directed, in writing, to Ganǫhkwásra⁷ Family Assault Support Services, P.O. Box 250, Ohsweken, Ontario, Canada N0A 1M0.

Sponsored by the Department of Canadian Heritage, Citizen's Participation & Multiculturalism and the Aboriginal Healing Foundation

Written/Edited by Stacy Tekonwanyahesen Hill for Ganǫhkwásra⁷ Family Assault Support Services
Illustrations by Raymond R. Skye

Library and Archives Canada Cataloguing in Publication

Hill, Stacy Tekonwanyahesen, 1976-
        Sonhatsi:wa = Your true self/ writer/editor, Stacy Tekonwanyahesen Hill; illustrator, Raymond R. Skye.

ISBN 0-9696470-5-0

1. Rape victims--Ontario--Biography. 2. Indians of North America--Violence against--Ontario. 3. Rape victims--Rehabilitation--Ontario. 4. Mental Healing.

I. Skye, Raymond R. II. Title. III. Title: Your true self.
E99.I69H54 2005
362.883'089'970713   C2005-902379-1

Ganǫhkwásra⁷ Publications

Ganǫhkwásra⁷ Family Assault Support Services
P.O. Box 250
Ohsweken, Ontario, Canada N0A 1M0
Telephone: (519) 445-4324
Fax: (519) 445-4825
Email: ganohkwasra@sixnationsns.com
www.ganohkwasra.com

This book is dedicated to the late Wilma General and Reva Bomberry, the founding Director of **Ganǫhkwásra'**, for their love and dedication to our people. Special acknowledgement also goes to the original **Ganǫhkwásra'** Steering Committee for their perseverance and commitment to bringing **Ganǫhkwásra'** (love among us) to our community.

First Words

Ohénton Karihwatéhkwen

Ohędǫ́ Gaihwadéhgǫh

The Thanksgiving Address is the basis for understanding the Haudenosaunee (Longhouse People/Iroquois) world view. It is the first words given to open and close all gatherings, meetings and ceremonies.

And so, to begin we extend our thanks, greetings and love for the people, that everyone is at peace.

We extend our thanks, greetings and love to our Mother, the Earth.

We extend our thanks, greetings and love to the waters on the earth.

We extend our thanks, greetings and love to the fish, in the waters he placed them.

We extend our thanks, greetings, and love to the plant life, the vegetables and fruit.

We extend our thanks, greetings and love to the medicines.

We extend our thanks, greetings and love to the free, wild animals.

We extend our thanks, greetings and love to the trees.

We extend our thanks, greetings and love to the birds.

We extend our thanks, greetings and love to the winds.

We extend our thanks, greetings and love to our Grandfathers, the thunders.

We extend our thanks, greetings and love to our Elder Brother, the Sun.

We extend our thanks, greetings and love to the Grandmother Moon.

We extend our thanks, greetings and love to the stars.

We extend our thanks, greetings and love to the Four Beings who watch over us from above.

We extend our thanks, greetings and love to the Peacemaker and Handsome Lake for all they have done for us.

Finally, we give our thanks, greetings and love to **Shonkwaya'tihson**, the one who made you.

This is all that I can do. And now it is done.

Our Hopes

It is the hope of the Board and staff of **Ganǫhkwásra'** *Family Assault Support Services that this book will reach people far beyond ourselves as an organization. We hope the stories within this book will touch the hearts of the people in our community, amongst the Haudenosaunee, across Turtle Island and one day across Mother Earth. Creator, we believe in the healing of the minds, bodies and spirits of all people. We believe in you. We believe in your love. Nya:wen for being our source of continual love, hope and healing.*

[Translation in the Mohawk Language courtesy of Tom Deer]

Aiá:wenhs ki ki:ken Kahiatóhsera ísi' nonkwanén:rati nienhén:we. Aiá:wens ki ne kí:ken okara'shón:a kén:en kahiá:ton aweriahsá:ke enkaié:na ne onkwe'shón:a ne kén:en onkwanonhstá:ton, ó:ni tsi ratí:teron ne Haudensaunee, ó:ni tsi na'tewataká:ron ne a'nó:wara kawé:note tánon enwenhniseraién:take tsi na'tewataká:ron ne iethi'nisténha ohwéntsa. Takwaia'tíhson tionkwehtáhkwen tsi sónhne. Tionkwehtáhkwen ne sanoronkwá:tshera. Niá:wen tsi tiótkon satká:was ne kanoronhkwá:tshera, kahskanéksera tánon kaie'wentásera.

[Translation in the Cayuga Language courtesy of Marjorie Henry]

Ayawéh né' nęgyéh oyadóhsrǫ:dǫ' ętsǫ́ hǫwéh héwe'
Ayawéh gí' nęgyéh gaga'shǫ'ǫh gahya:dó' hęga:ye' godęhehtrá ǫ́gweh
Ayawéh ní shęh dwanagré' né' Hadihnǫhsǫ́:ni
Né'ni'né' hodiyahsdóh Ganyahdę́ Gahwéhnǫ'
Wędǫhgwá' ohwejagwegǫ́h hę́:we'
Gyogwedahgǫ́h né' ęswadehsrǫ:ní' ǫgwanigohá' ne'ní' dwaya'dagéh ne'ní' shęh nidwaya'dó'dę:
Gyǫgwedahgǫ́h sqwayá'dihsǫh
Gyǫgwedahgǫ́h Sgwanǫ́hkwa'
Nyawéh desa'stohǫgyé' sadęnidaóhsra'

April, 2005

Atgǫ́nǫhǫnyǫh (I hold you in high esteem)

I would like to take this opportunity to acknowledge each individual who shared their healing journey and participated in the making of this book.

The courage and inner strength that each of you have taken to deal with the traumatic experiences you have encountered throughout your lifetime, is most admirable.

Each of you are gifts from the Creator and I truly believe that the strength you have taken to overcome the traumatic experiences only enhances, revitalizes and strengthens that inner beauty and spirit within you.

It is our hope that your story will touch the life of someone and empower them to overcome the trauma that was inflicted upon them.

Sa da dagyę́ na wa's (You take care of yourself)

Nya:weh (thank you)

Dusty

Doris Henry,
Director
Ganǫhkwásra' Family Assault Support Services

Sonhatsí:wa
Your True Self

Table of Contents

About this book   11

Planning for Safety While Reading   14

Poem— Sonhatsí:wa   17

"I healed in my own community"   19

Poem—Mother of the Earth   39

Heart Sandwich®   40

"The Creator blessed me with so much"   41

Poem—Looking Glass   59

Journal   60

"It wasn't always my fault"   61

Poem—Untitled   73

Pray or Meditate   74

"I just wanted to be loved"   75

Poem—My Fortress   87

Connect with creation   88

"I have found my voice"   91

Poem—Trapped   101

Release your emotions in a healthy way   103

"I am learning a new way of life"   105

Poem—I Forgive You   124

Contain your feelings in a safe place until you are able to address them   125

"I can stop leaving my body now"   127

Poem—The Mirror's Answer   141

Burn medicines that are for cleansing   143

"Today I'm more who the Creator sent me to be"   145

Poem— Forgiveness   165

Have a sea salt bath   166

"I hope it never has to happen to someone else"   167

Poem—What I need from you …   183

Sing or Chant   185

"No one is going to stop me from living my life"   187

Poem— The Monster Under My Bed   196

Have someone comb your hair   198

Ganọhkwásra' Family Assault Support Services   199

Sonhatsí:wa   213

The Healing Journey of First Nations People   227

Maintaining A Good Mind   232

What Is Sexual Assault?   234
What Is Consent?
Did you know?

If you have been sexually assaulted recently …   235
If you were sexually abused as a child …
If you are a male survivor of sexual abuse …

Flashbacks   237

Resources   239

We Would Love To Hear From You   241

Sonhatsí:wa Feedback Form   242

Acknowledgements 244

Closing 246

About This Book

"Sonhatsí:wa" is a word in the Mohawk language that refers to the true self. It literally means "you all by yourself" in the truest sense. To understand what that means think of yourself in a space, free from the influences of the world – people, creation, sound, colours, your physical body. Then ask yourself, what is left? What is it that is you? We believe the only thing that exists in that space is your connection to your higher power. Nothing else matters. You are only a spirit of Creator's love. Like a baby being born into this world, you are pure and complete. All of your goodness, your potential, your most natural state of being is in that image and that is who you truly are.

At **Ganohkwásra⁷**, we hope this book will touch the lives and hearts of people far and wide. We hope it will inspire individuals to gather their courage and take the first step on their path to healing that includes equality, caring, compassion and non-violence. We hope to encourage those individuals currently walking their healing path to continue. We understand at times it feels as though you've come to an impasse, that you don't have the strength left to get past yet another barrier or trauma. Our hope is that these heart-stories are what is needed to empower individuals to know they have the strength to do whatever it takes and more. Our true selves are always with us. We are confident that everyone can connect to who they are truly meant to be.

The original vision for this book grew from an increasing demand for culturally relevant, family violence/sexual assault information. The healing work undertaken by **Ganohkwásra⁷**, as well as statistics compiled from our Community Education services, have indicated that in order to be successful we need to be in charge of developing resources that reflect our needs as Onkwehonwe (First Nations) people. It was felt that we are in a unique position to share healing stories of pain, triumph and love with others seeking inspiration, hope and understanding. With the help of funds from Canadian Heritage: Citizen's Participation & Multiculturalism and the Aboriginal Healing Foundation, a Resource Development Worker was hired in June 2003. This worker immediately began research with traditional resource people in the Six Nations community to gather cultural teachings and oral traditions in regards to history, family, community and sexuality. Many of these teachings are included at the end of this book. We believe that these traditions bring an important element to this book, due to their significance to our people and to our community.

Past and present participants of **Sonhatsí:wa** (Sexual Assault Program) and **Saho'nikonrí:io'ne** (Mens' Program) were approached to participate in this book. They were honoured at the opportunity to help others by sharing their transformation from lives disrupted by sexual assault to becoming their true selves. The process for gathering these heart-stories has truly been a healing process for all involved, including the staff at **Ganohkwásra'**. Each participant was given a choice as to how they would tell their healing story in written form. Many chose to do some of their own writing, some tape-recorded themselves in the privacy of their own home while others met with the Resource Development Worker to share the details of their traumas and growth as they were recorded. From there, each participant worked with the Resource Development Worker and the Sexual Assault Program Supervisor to edit their story to the finished product you have here.

We would like to acknowledge the individuals who have shared themselves for the purposes of this book. It takes a great amount of courage and humbleness to share a piece of yourself for the benefit of others. The work and the tears you have put into your healing will be an inspiration to others. We have been honoured to work with each and every one of you.

For the protection and safety of the individuals who have participated in this book, each heart-story has been kept anonymous. It is not the identity of the person that is important, it is the message of healing they offer. Any names mentioned have been changed and at times personal details have been omitted.

A note about terminology

This book has been written from a First Nations perspective; however, it is specific to the community of the Six Nations of the Grand River. At **Ganǫhkwásra'** we believe it is important to use our languages to describe our people. Therefore, when referring to the people of the Six Nations Iroquois Confederacy we have used "**Haudenosaunee**" (Longhouse People or literally "they build houses"—Ho-dee-no-sho-nee). This is who we know ourselves to be. When referring to all original people of North America we have used "First Nations" as we are the first, or original, nations of this land. As well, you may see the word "**Shonkwaya'tihson**" or "**Shǫgwayadíhsǫh**" (Son-gwa-ya-dee-son) used throughout the text. This is how we refer to the Creator, "The One Who Made You."

Planning for Safety While Reading

Please be aware, the healing journeys that follow contain instances of sexual traumas that may be emotionally triggering for you, the reader. You may experience feelings of anger, fear, or sadness. You may have memories and overwhelming feelings associated with your own sexual abuse. You may also have strong feelings of empathy for the participants of the book that are hard for you to overcome. We strongly suggest you take measures to ensure your emotional safety while reading this book. The following are a few suggestions:

- Ask a friend to also read the book - Get together from time to time, talk about the book and support one another
- Take your time - read a bit then take a break from it
- Keep your feet on the floor and breathe deeply (techniques to keep you grounded)
- Talk to support people if needed
- Do some journaling
- Listen to a meditation tape

If you experience difficulties while reading this book please reach out for support. There are services available in most communities that offer support and counselling for issues of family violence and sexual assault. Throughout this book there are healthy strategies for managing overwhelming feelings you may experience. Try them. These will help to calm you and will enable you to manage any overwhelming feelings you may experience. They're simple, yet they work. There is also other helpful information, phone numbers and websites at the back of the book.

Identifying your feelings
The following are some examples of what you may experience as you are reading the stories within this book:

Anger - tension in your right shoulder, a sore jaw, grinding your teeth, raising your voice more, or being more easily frustrated

Fear - feeling shaky or trembling, having night sweats, having nightmares, feelings of anxiety, a sore lower back or a headache at the top of your head

Sadness - crying, feeling teary-eyed, feeling vulnerable, or feeling heavy in the chest/heart

The Importance of Breathing

Breathing has been suggested here as a grounding technique. Deep breathing is very important. Breathing from the lower belly is the correct way to breath. This is the way we all breath as infants when we came into the world and when we had no fear. Put your hands on your lower abdomen. As you breath in, your belly inflates or fills with air and you will see your hands move outward. As you let your breathe out, your belly will go back to normal and your hands will lower. You may feel like you are exaggerating your breathing because many of us have forgotten how to breath. Throughout life people experience fear and stop breathing with their full diaphragm. It would be good to practice this breathing technique as you read the sensitive areas of this book.

Through this work I am constantly reminded that we do have a Creator and I'm very grateful for that. This work has been very spiritual for me because of that. It always comes back to sharing the beliefs I have about our teachings, the traditions of our people. People I have worked with have wanted to hear about our culture because they're searching. They come here searching for who they are and what they are beyond the trauma; who they could have been. Then they do their grieving of that. They sort through their issues, and after doing their healing work around their traumas they find who they are, their true self.

Sexual Assault Counsellor,
Sonhatsí:wa Sexual Assault Program
Ganǫhkwásra' Family Assault Support Services

Sonhatsí:wa

Words drip from my hands like honey
Offering solace to those that seek shelter
from harsh realities.

Simple truths spoken,
agreements from another time,
honoured in their simplest form.

We will be our chosen self
and lovingly embrace authenticity,
as we feel the warmth of the Creator's breath
and the gentleness of his touch,
we understand the freedom to be ourselves.

Wa'osanę́go
Gayadago:wa 2003

"I healed in my own community"

My life before sexual trauma was innocent. I played sports. I tried to please my mom and dad. I was the oldest girl so I was always given the lecture about setting an example. That came from both of my parents. My brothers, sisters and I were safe. We played. We went fishing at the river. We went swimming. We had a garden. We worked pretty hard. I remember doing the assembly line bath; there was so many of us. We had a wash tub we had to do all of the bathing in. Thank goodness I was one of the older ones. I would have hated to be the baby and get a bath after five kids! I have lots of memories of catching fireflies outside at night in the summer, going after pollywogs in the creek. We'd chase the cows and get caught in the pasture when they were running toward us. We were kind of scared of them so we'd run and climb up a tree. Then we'd have to yell for our mother who would be outside hanging sheets. My mom and dad were together all that time.

I remember going up to my great-grandpa's house. That was a wonderful place, with the chickens, the barn, the horses, the gardens and the well we would draw water from. There were always a lot of people, always a lot of getting together. It was always clear that the kids played with the kids and the adults were with the adults. There are so many good memories. I would say there were ten years of good memories to sustain and reinforce in me that I was a kid.

When I was ten, things in my life drastically changed. My mom and dad separated. My mom had left us for a little while. My dad hired a babysitter to come and stay with us because he was an ironworker, working out of town. Our dad talked to us and told us that our mom might come back. He was crying. Things were happening that didn't feel good to me. Then, my dad left. Our mom told us he wasn't coming back. I didn't understand that because my dad always came back. He'd always come home from work. I couldn't understand why she was saying those mean things.

Different people started coming around and drinking at the house. I remember one time I caught my mother kissing another man. I was horrified. I was crying and wondering why my mother was kissing this man and who was he anyway? After that I began to realize something was going wrong with my family. When my tenth birthday came I had no birthday party. No recognition of it at all. That was awful, but I guess it was just another sign that things were falling apart.

In August, before school started that year, my mother packed us up and we moved to the other end of the reserve. We moved into a little wee, three room house. It was a big change from the big house we were used to living in. That's when I was raped. I used to be left alone to babysit my brothers and sisters. I was ten and we had a lot of younger ones. One night my uncle came into the bedroom. He turned the light on and said, "Get over." I was in the bottom bunk with my sister next to me. I said, "There's no room here." Then he said, "Well then, you get up and come with me." I didn't think anything. I only wondered why my uncle wanted me to go with him. My older brother was in the kitchen. My uncle sent him to look for a radio, then he turned to me and said, "Come on, we're going for a ride." He drove down a side road and he raped me. The last thing I can remember is him saying, "I'm going to kill you."

The next day, I woke up in my room and I thought it was a dream; it was a big horrible dream. I thought, "Here I am in my bed. Nothing happened. It was just a dream." Then I got up and my pajamas were all blood. Still, I thought I must have had an accident. I went to the outhouse and it really hurt when I peed. My mind just kept telling me it didn't happen. When I ran back to the house, I found my shoe on the step. I wondered why my shoe was out there and then things started to dawn on me that something really had happened to me. I don't know what I did for the next while but I never told anyone anything. Somehow I must have convinced myself that nothing happened.

Not quite a year later, when the weather had turned cold again, we were at a turkey shoot. My brother asked me if I wanted to shoot for him. Just then, this car pulled in. It was my uncle and two other guys. They came walking up to do the turkey shoot. I had this gun in my hand and I wanted to turn and shoot him. Actually, I did lower the gun but my brother was standing there. He grabbed the gun and said, "What are you doing? Where are you pointing that gun? Give me that gun. You're going to shoot someone." I don't remember much about that time in my life. There are big gaps I've never been able to get back. I don't remember starting school that year and I don't remember Christmas. It's like a big blank. It's gone and I don't really care to get it back.

That was in September and by mid-October we were taken to the Mush Hole [Mohawk Institute residential school]. I remember driving up to the Mush Hole. My sister, my brother and I were in the back seat. My mother said, "You kids are going to the Mush Hole because your damn father won't help me!" We just sat there. No one asked anything. I had no idea what she meant. All I could imagine was that my mother was going to go throw us into a hole of mush. We ate oatmeal and called it mush so I thought, "I hope I can swim a long time because I'm going to have to hold us up."

When we got to the residential school, we settled into our lockers and our dorms. There were some women who were nice and smiley, until no other adults were around. Then they were pretty harsh and mean.

There were children there who didn't speak English. They were Cree. I remember I had never come across anyone who spoke a different language. I was used to hearing Mohawk, Oneida, Cayuga and our languages around here but I had never come across the Cree language. It was very different. Somehow we knew we couldn't communicate. I started to see that people were meaner to the kids who didn't speak English, even the other kids were meaner to them.

I remember one day, this girl Sarah was told to tell the Cree kids to make their beds. She tried to explain to them but the woman instructing her was getting more and more frustrated. Finally, the woman went over and back-handed Sarah across the face. Sarah was crying; she wasn't even thirteen years old. The woman was hollering, "You're not telling them! I can tell by the look on their faces that they don't understand. You tell them!" Then, Sarah caught her breath, flipped her hair back and said "There's no word for bed. We don't have beds. I don't know how to say it." It was so very unreal to me that she was getting punished for a language barrier that wasn't her fault.

When I got to work in the dinette room for the staff, one of the older girls showed me how to set the table. She would say, "Now you have to do it this way. Put the glasses here, the dishes here." When we were pretty much done she says, "Okay, this is the last piece." She brought in the hot tray with a big dish of potatoes on it. She said, "The last thing you have to do before they come in to eat is this." She picked up a big scoop of mashed potatoes, spit in the dish of potatoes and put the rest back. She says, "Do it!" So I scooped it out, spit and put it back down. Then she says, "Good, now you're one of us." That was my initiation: shit on the staff. They shit on us and we get even with them and that was what the institutionalization was all about. It was them against us. How was I ever to feel like someone was taking care of us and nurturing us when everything was about survival? It wasn't about people taking care of children. It was about children surviving the harsh reality of where they were, the hierarchal system of power they lived in and even having to defend themselves against other kids.

The senior girls "ruled the roost." One of the ways they did that was by having gangs. They would have girls fight for them, clean for them, get food for them, or steal for them. If they had a rival with another senior girl, sometimes instead of having a direct fight they would have their gang go after someone in the other girl's gang. It was not unusual at all for fights to be going on in the dorms, in the basement. Sometimes there were demands like, "You have to start a fight with a girl while you're going over to school today." If it wasn't done you would get beat up. It was all very manipulative and violent. The whole institution was a system of power and control.

The first time I had to fight with one of the girls in the bathroom I didn't know what was going on. One of the older, tough girls says, "Go ahead. You'll be alright. You're one of mine now." I thought, "I'm one of your what?" I was sitting on the edge of the toilet trying to figure out what was going on when this girl comes in and just bops me across the face, knocking me down on the floor between the toilet and the wall. The older girl was still standing there and she says, "See, you've got to fight or you'll get your ass kicked every day." At that moment something happened inside of me. All of this hate and anger came out of me. I think part of it was the rape, part was the resentment of my mother, and part was the confusion of being in this horrible place. When we were finished there was blood all over the walls, chipped teeth, and hair pulled out. The senior girl whose gang I was part of at the time said in an approving tone, "Good." I thought, *That's good, eh? All I have to do is fight like an animal, claw, dig, gouge, and bite, to be good? What a different world this is.* I hadn't asked for this and by that time I was pretty pissed off that I had gotten thrown in there.

The leader of our gang had a little crew from Six Nations and she even had us fight against each other. It was no different for the boys. Actually, I think the boys had it worse. They had to make swords out of boards. They'd shave them off to a point and they'd fight. There was a barn in the back. The boys would fight to either take over or defend the barn. I heard of one boy who was kicked to death by the other boys. He was in my classroom and all of a sudden he was gone. The rumours were he was kicked and his spleen broke. After that it became a joke. The older boys would say, "Do that for me or I'll kick your spleen open." Two of those boys who were involved in that actually got killed in a car accident shortly after they were released from the Mush Hole.

The sexual trauma I experienced at the residential school was witnessing it. I knew what was happening to those girls and that was traumatizing enough for me. I don't know what month this might have been but it was the day the Beatles made their debut on the Ed Sullivan Show in '63. Everyone remembers the first appearance of the Beatles in an exciting way but I remember them in a very different way.

I remember being in this little TV room in the basement. All these Cree girls were there. The Minister came into the playroom. I was mulling over why all these Cree girls were going crazy and screaming at the TV when they couldn't understand what those guys were saying. The Minister pulled these handcuffs out of his pocket. I was really watching him because by that time I was pretty hyper-alert to men. Some of the Cree kids were interested but the other kids were just staring straight ahead. They didn't want anything to do with what was going on. I was thinking, *This is weird.* Then, this girl who must have been around twelve or thirteen, went walking over and said, "What are these for?" The Minister said, "I'll show you how they work." He put one handcuff on her wrist and one on his. Then he took her into the back room.

It was uncanny to me because a lot of the other kids didn't even bother to look over. I figured this out later but they must have known what was going on. Some of them were watching but nobody made a move to do anything. Nobody ran to get any adults for help. Nobody hollered. Nobody said no. There were certainly enough of us girls there. There must have been about thirty of us. We could have ganged up on him. I think it was that white collar. Everything he did must be okay because he was a preacher in Sunday school, in the church.

She was kind of laughing because he was tickling her to make her laugh. That room back there was where the house mother did her paper work but she wasn't back there so he used his key to get in. I could hear keys fumbling. He opened the door, pulled her in, and shut the door. Then I could hear her screaming and then nothing. That was enough to trigger me. I knew what was going on. In my mind I was screaming, "Why the hell doesn't somebody do something?" But I couldn't move. I froze. I was terrified. I got this overwhelming feeling that no place was safe. I started to think it was going to happen to me again. I knew what he did to that girl and I began to wonder who was going to come after me.

I saw another young girl, maybe around eleven or twelve years old, try to commit suicide. She tried to poison herself then cut her wrists with the lid of a can. We were supposed to be cleaning in the library and all of a sudden she started mixing the cleaning fluid together. Then she says, "Come on, drink some with me. I'm going to die today." I just said, "You go right ahead, that stuff stinks." I was in another part of the room so I didn't see what she did but I remember there was a can sitting there with a jagged lid. She must have used that part of the can to cut her wrists enough to bleed because the next time I saw her she was bleeding. I remember seeing her just standing there with blood dripping down her hands at her sides. She had this real stunned look on her face. Her eyes were just kind of glazed over and her mouth was opened. I went and got one of the house mothers down the hall. She came but she didn't have a very big reaction. She just stood there and told me to leave. That was the last time I saw that girl. By that point in my life, I had already learned not to ask questions and I never asked about her. It wasn't until years in therapy that I recovered that memory. I realized it was related to all the types of trauma I saw at the residential school.

When I came home from the Mush Hole I knew I was different. I had changed after months of living there, seeing other kids raped and trying to commit suicide, having to fight my way through every day to survive. I could never go back to being an innocent little girl. Other girls my age could play and skip and have fun and talk about this or that. To me that was not a part of my reality anymore. I just knew I no longer fit in that world.

We went back to the same house my uncle had taken me from and raped me. It was hard to be there. A couple of other men tried to attack me and I stabbed one with a kitchen knife. He said, "You're crazy, I just wanted to kiss you." I said, "I know what you wanted." They were family members too, older drinking buddies of my mom and her boyfriend. I had become a little hard-core, meaning I knew how to take care of myself. I was gaining some confidence in my anger. My anger was going to protect me. That wasn't a conscious thought but looking back now, I can see the transition I went through. For a while I was this little girl, huddled in the fetal position, scared and anxious, almost wanting to get sick when I was alone in a room with a man. Then I changed. I became very angry, aggressive and violent.

By the time I was twelve, I was drinking every weekend and had become quite sexually active. It wasn't really about the sex though. It was more about gaining some kind of control. I would if I felt like it and I would if I didn't. It didn't matter if I liked them or if they were older. Nothing mattered. I had tried to tell my mother that her brother had raped me. She just looked at me real funny and said, "Oh my god. No man will ever want you now." My sexuality was already completely distorted by the rape so my mother's reaction didn't help matters. I started to classify girls as those who were dirty and those who were virgins. That was my own classification. In my mind, I was with the dirty girls, so I acted like it. I had just changed so much and I knew I wasn't my dad's little girl anymore.

I quit school by the time I was fifteen. I was drinking quite a bit and my mother would say, "You're going to kill yourself. I can't stand to watch that." So I thought, "Well, you don't have to," and I left. I lived with a guy off and on for about three years, between the ages of fifteen to eighteen. I moved around between different cities. It didn't really matter to me. I look back on it now and I was just like a gypsy. I didn't care where I stayed. I remember I used to piss off a lot of women. They would get pretty mad at me, and with reason. If any man showed an interest in me I would have this attitude as if I was in charge; I'll decide if I'll let you have some of me. After that, sex became a weapon. It wasn't really sex.

I remember lots of times waking up in the oddest place after having been so drunk. I would wake up under beds or in the backs of cars with all the doors locked. I realized later that I would get drunk then I must have hid myself before passing out. It was a very, very shameful part of my life. I don't know what I was looking for. I think I just wanted to feel safe.

I think my low point was just the wandering, wishing I could reclaim some part of the better years of my life. I had become suicidal at the time. I can't remember how I thought I might kill myself; pills I guess. I was too chicken to jump off a bridge, although it had occurred to me. One time, I jumped out of a car that was going down the road. I remember my head hitting the pavement and coming to in the hospital. Still, I never ever turned to drugs and I never turned to prostitution. I never did any of those and I think that was something I prided myself for.

When I was about eighteen, I had gotten tired of the bar scene and the pool halls. There were some adults around who would say, "What are you doing to yourself? You've got to do better than this. You're just a young girl and you seem like a smart girl. You have so much more to offer. You can do better."

Some women started to ask me to babysit for them so I did and I liked it. I liked putting the little ones to bed and taking care of them. Deep down I think it made me feel good knowing they were safe. I would tell their parents, "If you're too drunk to come back after them, leave them and come get them in the morning." There were some kids I got quite close to. I think that must have been a turning point for me because I realized I liked kids.

When I was about nineteen, I had enough of the abusive relationship I was in. Babysitting those kids got me to start thinking I wanted something different for myself so I went home. I went home for two weeks but I could not stand being in my mother's house. She would wake me up and say, "You get up now. You've got dishes to do." I remember thinking, "What am I doing here?" So I moved out again.

I moved in with one of my aunt's. She was going to school at the time. I stayed with her and helped with her kids while she went to school. I watched her get up everyday, work damn hard with the books, and go off to class. I'd watch the kids, she'd come home, cook supper and hit the books again. When the weekends would come, she'd go out maybe one night and that would be it. Here I was out Thursday to Sunday. I started thinking she was on to something. She talked to me about why she wanted to go to school, get a job and take care of her kids. It made sense to me, something clicked. I asked, "Could I do that?" She said, "Sure you could" and she helped me get back in school. I took a secretarial course.

I was twenty-one when I finished that course. At that point in my life I had started to slow down. I wasn't as sexually active. I just turned off of sex altogether. It just didn't interest me at all. Then I met this guy, after I was almost through my year in school and we moved in together. He was nice. He really liked me. It didn't matter that I didn't really like him. At the wedding my aunt came to me and said, "You don't really have to do this." I said, "I know." But it was another turning point for me because I knew I had to change what I had been doing. I thought marrying him was the right thing to do. So we got married in June and six months later, I was pregnant.

Being pregnant was the best time in my life. I was twenty-two years old when I had my first child and I was okay. I felt normal. I had a house to clean. I had a man to cook for. He was working then. He didn't drink very much. I didn't care to drink at all throughout my pregnancy nor did I smoke. I didn't want to do anything that would harm my baby. Don't ask me how I knew that. I think it was my grandpa. Years earlier he had told us, "There will be something wrong with your kids if you drink and smoke." Things were good. Even sex had become okay. I wasn't using it for some other purpose anymore. Yet, in my sex life, I felt I could never say no. I felt like I was obligated. Still, that was okay because I never really felt anything about sex. It was just sex.

A couple of years later I had my second child. I started to find out I was having trouble with people in my life after I had my kids. I became very irritable. I didn't care. I'd start arguments. It was like I couldn't stand peace and quiet. I argued constantly with my mother. She would cry and say, "Why do you treat me this way?" I hadn't put it together. I hadn't had any counselling or anything yet so I didn't understand it myself. I was just very bitter and resentful and hateful. I started drinking again. When I'd drink I'd fight with my husband. I'd fight with anybody. That was the rage coming back again although I didn't know that at the time.

My husband and I decided to move to the States. I think we were trying to salvage our family; we were trying to pretend everything was okay. I don't think we even realized our marriage was in trouble but we started drinking more and fighting more. He was running around on me and I was running around on him. We were still trying to patch things together but I didn't have anything left in me to do that. I couldn't. I was just trying to save my kids from losing their dad. It had been horrible for me when my dad left; all hell broke loose. I didn't want that to happen to my kids.

So we moved to the States and I started going to school there. One day my husband left to go up north and get a job. He was gone for two weeks. The rent was coming due and I had no money. I had no idea how to get money. The phone was cut off so I went to a pay phone and called home to my mom. She said, "What the hell is going on? Your husband's home drinking and running around, telling everyone that you sold the kids and you won't come home." That was horrible. I had already bounced back from one horrible period in my life; I wasn't quite prepared to bounce back from another one. I went and drank. I managed to still wander back and forth to classes. A neighbour was more or less taking care of my children. I remember calling the bus station one day and asking how much it would cost for bus tickets to Buffalo. I had figured if I could get the kids to Buffalo, someone else could come and get them. I was consciously planning to put my children on a bus and send them back to Buffalo alone because I thought they were better off without me. I didn't have anything to offer them and I believed if they didn't have a father, they had nothing.

One day, a Native woman came into my class to announce a new program. It was counselling. If anybody had any kind of problems they could go and see her. So I went to see her. Finally, for the first time in my life I started to pour out what was really going on with me. In our conversation she said some things that were very simple but quite profound.

"Do you drink?"

"Yeah."

"What do you have in your life that's more important than the drinking?"

"My kids."

"If you want your kids more than you want drinking, I can help you."

"What do I have to do?"

"Stop drinking."

She gave me this card. It was about AA and a treatment program where I could stay in school. She helped me get into the program. I went to school during the day and counselling at night. They even got me babysitters. Again, things were turning around. In that counselling I faced everything; my childhood, sexual abuse, the whole bit. I also got to meet other people who were struggling with the same things. It was a relief to know my struggles weren't that unusual. There were a lot of us who had poor marriages or a broken marriage. I was really proud to see a lot of women were in recovery for their children.

I came home after being three years sober. I got back together with my husband for about a year but he continued to drink. I went to see a lady to have my fortune told. She told me she saw a parting of ways. That's what ended up happening; my husband and I divorced. I was all by myself for about nine years but it didn't really bother me except maybe at Christmas time. What was more important was that I was keeping my children safe. My children were never abused, except verbally by me; I could be quite a yeller. I stuck by my kids. I liked it. I was very proud of the fact that I sobered up for them. Even when they started drinking I would tell them, "I don't want you to drink. It took your dad and it doesn't add anything to anyone's life." Then I realized, I had to let them go and make their own choices.

I really looked for healing. I sought it out. I had started to cope with things but there was still a lot there. My parenting, my education, my jobs were things that were all helping me to get through but I realized I was still having problems with relationships and I hadn't really dealt with all of the sexual abuse. I had done enough of the alcohol counselling to see how the abuse contributed to my drinking but I knew I had to work on a lot more things other than drinking. It was more about what I believed was right and wrong, my values.

I knew I had a pretty violent past, being abused as well as being abusive, so I went to **Ganohkwásra'**. I found exactly what I needed with a counsellor in the sexual assault program there. I swear that woman is a million years old! She certainly seems like it in her spirit. She helped me to heal by showing me bad things happen to good people. She was so thorough and consistent. She was so focused on my healing, on me telling my story, on me being able to say, "This is what happened to me and it was so wrong. I was just a kid."

What happened to me was a horrible thing but through the counselling at **Ganohkwásra'** I know there are so many of us who have gone through it. When someone has been raped, when someone is sexually abused and traumatized by seeing it all around them, the whole world no longer feels safe and this survival mechanism kicks in. In therapy I was able to see how anger was my protection. As a child, I had gone from complete safety and protection to living in fear of what would happen next. I started accumulating all this rage towards my mother because I blamed her for the traumas I experienced. I blamed her for my rape. I was more enraged at my mother than I was at the person who raped me. I blamed her for putting us in the Mush Hole and leaving us to experience the hell that it was. I had to work through that just as much as I did the rape. I know I shouldn't be angry at my mom because she did do the best she could. I truly believe if she had known what was going to happen the night I was raped, or when she left us at the Mush Hole, she would have protected me but she couldn't because she was dealing with her own stuff.

I believe my anger, my rage, and keeping people away was the best thing for me back then. I needed that protection but after a while, the anger started to work against me. It started to affect how I was with people. I would hurt people and I didn't care about their feelings. It was all about protecting my own feelings and not caring about anybody else's. I still do it sometimes with my feelings. If I have a not-so-good relationship with somebody I know a big part of it is mine but I also know it's the other person too. I just try to remember I don't know what their issues are. I don't know what they've gone through. I don't know how they've learned to survive. There is just so much stuff going on out there.

At **Ganọhkwásra**[7], I realized the anger was also keeping me from what I really wanted, which was to get along with people, to have a happy life, to feel good. I was keeping myself stuck by hanging on to the anger. My counsellor helped me to see I didn't need it anymore. I let it go and I was even able to forgive my mother. I still have to work on that from time to time. Every time I start to feel the anger building up I have to stop and soften it and forgive. I've got too much life to live yet. I have too many people in my life I care about to carry that around anymore.

What really helped me in my therapy, was this one day of just giving up the control and allowing myself to do emotional release work.* My counsellor had asked me if I wanted to try screaming to let go of the fear I was carrying. At first I was resistant. "Scream?" I asked, "What the hell good is screaming? Don't make me scream for crying out loud. I can't do this." But I did. I trusted her that much. We tried it over and over again. It was a gradual process. Finally, one day I just let go and I screamed. I screamed until I couldn't scream anymore and I cried until I couldn't cry anymore. I went back to the time I was raped. It was so horrible. My counsellor held me as I screamed so I felt I was still safe. I was okay. I wasn't going anywhere. I wasn't going to explode. I wasn't going to disintegrate. Then, using spirit work, my great-grandpa stepped out from behind the door and his hand touched my shoulder. I was saved. He saved me. I realized he had been there all along. I just didn't know how to reach out.

From that experience, I recognized there were safe people in my life. My dad and my great-grandpa had always been a good part of my life. They never harmed me. In that one session, I learned how to reconnect with my grandpa and I found out the significance of the good memories in my life. Pulling out the good, the positive, was such a key part of my healing. Before therapy I didn't remember anything really good. To me, my whole world was all about the bad, the evil, how to survive and I forgot about the good. I really forgot about having some kind of balance, acknowledging that it wasn't just the bad things that shaped me. There were good things too like the way my grandpa would tell me things. One time he said, "Oil and water." He was standing by the wood stove. He poured some water in a mason jar. The water and oil separated. He said, "See that? That's just what the booze and family life are like. The two will never mix." I didn't understand what he was telling me then. I recovered that memory in therapy. Then I was able to understand the significance of that teaching. So my healing has been a lot about putting balance back into my life, pulling back those good memories.

My counsellor also taught me how to use those good memories of my childhood to help me today. She helped me to recall a place at my grandpa's house, where his chair was by the

---

* For a brief description of emotional release work refer to "Psychodramatic Bodywork" on p.203

tree, outside. The barn was back there where we used to go and get the eggs. I would feel so safe in that spot. I can see it in my mind and I can go there anytime. But now I go as a woman. I don't go as a little girl anymore. I recovered that part of me. I was a child and now I am an adult. I have grown so much. Today I work with children and I also have children of my own.

Finding the stories of our people, our history, the Code of Handsome Lake, stories of our origin, the dances, our songs, our teachings, had to happen for me. It was a big part of my healing. That is the foundation for who I really am. I've always felt that since I was abused, traumatized and raped, I was knocked off my spiritual path. It wasn't just my sexuality and my personality. It was my whole spiritual path. So now I'm reclaiming that. I am learning who I am and who we are as a people. It's so empowering to know I can do that right here, in our community, because that process began for me at Ganǫhkwásraʼ.

My counsellor was so gentle and so subtle in the way she helped me reconnect with my spirit. It was through using the water drum, the songs, and the music. After a hard session, she would comb my hair to help me to release the grief I was carrying. Sometimes, we would just have quiet times when we would sit on the floor or in the grass. She told me stories like the story of Hiawatha and how he lost his girls. There is great healing in that story. She talked about the spirit of our people. There are so many significant stories in our history. It's great to learn about what happened to our people and how we have continued to survive. All of that is real. That's who we really are. It's a really good feeling, to be able to know who we really are and to be able to understand our connections with each other.

For me, there's something about my sense of home that healed too. That whole experience of my home falling apart has been healed. I have a home again, it's called community. I'm very proud to be working here. I'm just so proud to see all the people who are a part of this dynamic of healing and changing. I feel it. It's there and it's very real. It's not healing to be something we're not. We're getting back on track. The best part of it all is that maybe this trauma happened to me in the community, but I healed in my own community. That's something I'm very proud of. My own people were able to help me heal. I didn't have to go somewhere else to be fixed and come back. I healed right here, with my own people. I think that it's so powerful to know we're here for each other. We just have to reach out and open ourselves to connecting with the people who can help us.

I have been with my current husband for thirteen years now. I think that through him and my dad, I have restored my faith that not all men are monsters. I can see now that people make their choices. I've matured. Today I know I've always been a good person. I've always been trying to find my way and I really think I have found it. I have been able to reach out and reconnect with the good people in my life. I can feel real feelings. I can feel joy of seeing a new grandbaby. I can grieve in a healthy way. I can feel joy to see my children win a game and I can share their frustration when they don't. I have changed. I am healing.

Sometimes, I still get quite upset that if those things had not happened to me, I would be different. I would not have had to learn to live with how that changed my whole way of being. But, the fact is it did happen and I am who I am today because of it. So now I accept the few long term effects that surface from time to time. For a long time, I didn't come out of sleep how you normally would. I would wake up suddenly, startled. When I'm under a lot of stress it comes back even yet. I realize today with all of my therapy that it's something I've learned to do or it's something my body has done because of the trauma. I think the last time it happened was when my daughter was turning ten. I had a lot of flashbacks that year. Now I just continue to believe in my connection with Creator. When I have that startled awakening, I know I'm not in a good place. But, I also know I can reclaim my connection again. I know where to go. I know how to get my balance back again.

On a final note, for those people who have not yet experienced what **Ganohkwásra'** has to offer, you don't know what you're missing. If you have been raped, please remember, it's happened to me too. If you haven't told anyone yet or started to talk about it, now is the time. If you're a residential school survivor, the advice is the same for you. Tell your story, even if it's just in the privacy of a counsellor you trust. Don't worry that you might have kept it quiet for a long time, anytime is the right time for the truth. If people just pretend it never happened to them, it's going to go on. Nothing is going to be healed until all the truth comes out.

By talking about the traumas I have experienced, I have seen how they affected me. I am happy there are people who are not afraid to tell their story but how many stories haven't been told? By sharing my story in my community I have learned there are so many of us. We've all experienced the same pain and fears but we've also shared the same desire to heal, to change, and to improve our lives not only for ourselves but also for the lives of those around us. To me, this is just my way of giving back to my community.

Mother of the Earth

You took my hand and heard what I did not tell you.
Slowly I walked toward you,
Daring to hope for a peaceful end,
To a lifelong search for serenity and peace.

Child-like and afraid I ran from you; let me go.
I wished for you to chase me, find me.
Gently you uncovered my hiding places,
Amidst the tears we found horrible memories, horrible places.

I watched as you burned sacred tobacco, whispering a prayer.
Tightly, but so gently, you held me as I cried and screamed,
You let me fight the release of my pain and despair,
Staying beside me as I thrashed and kicked and wailed.

I wanted to remain to share my new dreams and future life,
To remain abreast, nurtured as a child by a mother's love.
Yet comes a time for new growth, for others, young and old,
So you gently nudged me from the nest; to stand and walk strong,
An adult-child healed by a Mother of the Earth.

From the Heart to the Healer, 2001

Heart Sandwich®

The Heart Sandwich® is a grounding technique (a technique that helps a person stay in the present) developed by Susan Aaron. Place one or both hands over your heart and breathe deeply. Allow yourself to feel the warmth of your hand on your heart. With your hand on your heart, feel the movement of your chest as you slowly inhale and exhale. As you breath in, and gently slow yourself down, take in the warmth and calmness. By using this technique you are working with the heart chakra to calm and reassure this emotional centre of energy. (We have seven major "chakras" in our body which are centres of physical, mental, emotional and spiritual energy.)

"The Creator has blessed me with so much"

"The Creator has blessed me with so much."

Most of the recollections I have as a little boy, are when I was around the age of three and a half or four. I can't remember a whole lot but from what little I do remember I seemed to be fairly happy. I remember being home with my sister before she went to kindergarten. She's a year and a half older than me. After my sister went to school I spent a lot of time with my mother at home, around the house. I spent my days playing around the house and watching cartoons while my mom did housework. We'd be inside and outside depending on what needed to be done. I would have to take naps in the afternoon and I didn't like that very much. I'd get to go with her whenever we had to go shopping or we went to visit my grandmother. Those memories with my mother are very happy and very loving memories. I look back fondly on that part of my life.

My earliest memory of any sexual experiences was one time while visiting a female cousin of mine. We got naked and got under the covers. We were considerably young. I would guess that we were around four or five-ish. It was before I was going to school. I don't know if we learned that from what we saw or experienced but I guess we just thought it was natural and appropriate. We were playing house, kissing and fondling one another. Both of our mothers came upstairs at the same time and caught us. They were horrified and for quite some time we didn't have any more visits with that particular cousin. There were no bad feelings between the parents but I think there was a lot of shame and embarrassment.

Not long after that I was sexually abused as a child. It was in my home by a male cousin. He would stay overnight on the weekends. He lived away. His family lived off the reserve. They would come home on the weekends and in the summertime so I didn't see a whole lot of them. I never really liked that cousin. He and his older brother were kind of mean to me so I didn't really like them at first. He was a couple of years older than me and at that age kids can be bullies. He was sort of like that to me. We did get along here and there after I became familiar with him, but still we fought a lot throughout our childhood.

The first time he abused me he was staying overnight at

our house. My sister and I shared a room. We had bunk-beds. She would sleep on the top and I would sleep on the bottom or vice versa. When my cousin would stay overnight he would sleep in the same bed with me. It was then that I recall him feeling me up and rubbing up against me like mocking anal intercourse. As kids we called it "humping." Then he went down and performed oral sex on me. That was kind of the beginning. I didn't really know what was going on and I wasn't really scared. I just felt kind of stunned or confused. I remember feeling like it wasn't a natural thing. This was new to me so I had never had anybody tell me that it was wrong. I guess at the time I just accepted it as normal but it really didn't feel normal.

Those sexual experiences with my cousin happened frequently enough, pretty much every time he stayed over. If we were near one another I could expect that it would happen. It almost became game-like to us. I knew if he was going to stay overnight he was going to do to me what he did to me. It didn't always happen just at night either, it occurred during the day too, anytime he had the chance. I didn't really like the things my cousin did. Often there were times I was raped or forced into sexual activities. I was coerced by intimidation or by verbal threats, threats of physical beatings or physical intimidation or mental or emotional blackmail or just being tricked into engaging in the activities. He just wanted to have sex, basically every chance we got and he always had to have his way. The older I got the more I didn't like it. And the older I got the more he would want me to reciprocate the activities on him, perform oral sex on him. I thought it was completely gross and didn't like that. Getting into the ages of seven to ten, I started to like it less and less. By that time, I had come to the understanding that what we were doing wasn't acceptable.

There were times in our childhood that my cousin would abuse my sister as well and another female cousin who was basically the same age as my sister. The four of us ended up having a secretive kind of sexual club. We would always play doctor or play house and I guess we considered it normal. Still, we knew we had to sneak around and be secretive about it. The parents couldn't find out so I guess in a sense we knew it was bad. At the same time, we thought it was good or fun because even at a young age there was a sense of sexual gratification that we experienced. Although I didn't have sexual relations with my sister there were instances when we were involved in the same activities. Typically I was having a lot of sexual activity with my female cousin, the one who was the same age as my sister. We would act grown up and say we were going to get married to one another. We kissed a lot and were sexual with one another pretty much any time we stayed overnight, whether we stayed at my grandmother's where she lived or we stayed at my house.

As I grew older my sexual experiences and activities grew as well. I would often engage in sexual activities with male friends of mine, childhood friends that would stay overnight. We would touch each other and explore one another's bodies thinking it was just normal. What else was I to think? That's what I had learned. Whether I was the teacher to them or they experienced the same thing and we just brought our experiences together, I don't know. It was less frequent with them obviously than with my cousins. Actually, it was quite rare but it did indeed happen.

There were times when we as kids did get caught by our parents but with parents of that time, common practice was to sweep it under the rug, turn a blind eye, live in denial. We would get scolded and told not to do that sort of thing, maybe even a slight licking. They would be mad at us and we would be punished or grounded for a short period. Yet, I don't remember our parents sitting us down and talking to us about how inappropriate it was. Actually, I do remember those talks a couple of times but they weren't of great detail or with any great emphasis. Damn it! It should have happened; we should have been taught.

From the sexual trauma of my childhood I learned that it was okay to have sex. If I wasn't hurting anybody or hitting anybody or causing anybody to cry, it wasn't bad. It was a good thing. That really distorted my views on sexuality and I became highly sexually dysfunctional at a really young age because I thought it was okay to do this. I guess I normalized those experiences. I made it normal. I thought everybody did it. I didn't know it then but I rationalized it. Now I know it was my unconscious survival instincts kicking in so I could survive the trauma.

My cousin also taught me about masturbation, self-gratification. I practiced that fairly regularly as a young child and into my teen years. My mindset was if I wanted sexual gratification I would just do it. So if I wasn't having sex with my cousins, the next best thing was to self gratify myself through masturbation. With that came a tremendous amount of guilt and shame. It was very easy for me to hate myself for it. I learned very early that I had to hide, that was something you didn't let anyone know about. If you did that, you couldn't let your parents or older siblings or anyone older than you find out. I would use that to brutalize myself emotionally and mentally and just felt a lot of great shame and disgrace. I obsessively beat myself up about it because I was so ashamed of it. I wonder now how I made it through my childhood without really hurting myself or even killing myself. I felt bad to be hiding and sneaking around like that. Yet I just wanted to have those minutes of joy or bliss. Then I would go to great lengths to beat myself up again, emotionally, mentally and spiritually. The same vicious cycle over and over and over again. I think if addictive drugs were available to me then, I would have been a childhood drug addict.

I was really highly dysfunctional for almost all of my life. It wasn't like there was childhood, adolescence then adulthood. I was a teenager, an adolescent all the way through so there were many times when I did a lot of things that weren't proper or healthy or socially acceptable when it came to sex and society as a whole. I used those instances to beat myself down again, to belittle myself and hate myself. I held myself in such contempt. I revelled in my contempt for myself because I could do it so easily. I could hate myself so easily and punish myself so very effectively in my mind and in my thoughts. I did it on a regular basis, on a daily basis. Beginning in my childhood and throughout my life, I always felt negative about myself. I guess this thinking was given birth through the relationship I had with my father.

To me, my father was very hard to please. I was always wanting acceptance from him, wanting his love, affection, his approval yet never feeling in my own mind that I ever got that from him. I was afraid of him. He was a very controlling and domineering man. He was a strict disciplinarian so he hollered a lot. I got a lot of spankings, whippings and beatings. He'd say I was a bad bugger and in my own head I would think that I was bad. I felt that I never did anything right, that I was a bad person. I believed I wasn't worth anything; I was stupid. I was dumb. I was an idiot. I didn't use my mind. I didn't use my head. I always did the wrong thing. I was just an all around bad person. It was a very painful experience for me to go through my life with that mindset.

Apart from my self-loathing, I was also very sexually dysfunctional and promiscuous throughout my teenage years and my twenties. I had multiple, multiple partners. I cheated on my girlfriends very often. In all honesty, I cheated as often as I could. The majority of the time it was when I was out drinking but I did it when I was sober as well, without the effects of drugs or alcohol. That really affected me because I learned to find a form of self-importance or self-validation through sexual activity with other people. I thought that if someone had sex with me or if someone kissed me or showed me attention or they liked me, I was important. That validated for me that I was attractive and I was somebody or something to someone.

Another contributing factor was that, in my case, my primary perpetrator was male. As a result, later on it created a lot of anxiety and turmoil for me. Because of my self loathing tendencies, I used that as something else to beat myself up about. I didn't like men or want to be with them but because of my abuse I had a lot of same-sex experiences. In an attempt to distance myself from the reality of my past I was with as many women as I could be. The truth is I love women and their bodies, maybe just a little too much because I was with so many.

I hid in the sexual dysfunction and the promiscuity quite a bit and in the alcohol as well. Those things really prevented me from growing as a person and learning about myself. Every time I cheated on my girlfriends I tortured myself. The satisfaction and gratification were only instantaneous. The afterglow was very short. It wouldn't take long for me to feel guilty and hate myself even more. That's pretty much how my life went repeatedly throughout my teenage years and into my adulthood, up until as recent as the late spring and summer of 2003.

There were many occasions when I imposed my needs or desires on women a little more than I should have. Unfortunately, I violated women and the sacredness of a woman's right to say no. I always knew it wasn't right or I shouldn't do that but then I would think, "It's just sex. It's just sex." I was doing what I had learned at an early age; I was sexually gratifying myself. I wouldn't hit these women or harm them physically. I wouldn't threaten them but I would urge them and plead with them to have sex with me or let me have my fun. I would say, "Come on, let's just do it." I put out a lot of verbal peer pressure to have intercourse, to go all the way. I knew that wasn't appropriate behaviour. I knew I had to respect the other person's body or their decision. I knew no meant no. To look back on it I don't take much pride in myself during those times.

As a result of masturbating often throughout my adolescence and teenage years I had a problem with premature ejaculation, which didn't do a whole lot for my self-esteem or my self-confidence. I was insecure with my girlfriends about whether I lasted long enough. Also, being that I was so sexually promiscuous there would be times that I would be with experienced women and I would reach my heightened pleasure a lot sooner than they would. Then I would hear comments like, "Are you done already?" It was an awful experience to hear that.

I had a lot of insecurities when I was with my girlfriends. If they were smiling or talking to other guys when we were out drinking or partying, or if I thought they looked too long or too much at a guy, I would think that they were going to go out and be with those guys. I thought they were going to cheat on me because I wasn't man enough, or good enough. So those insecurities just added to my dysfunction. On one hand I had a lot of experience and therefore had a lot of self-confidence in my ability to satisfy a woman, yet on the other hand I had all of those insecurities.

It was very hard for me to get through my dysfunction. It caused a lot of problems within my relationships. The first time I actually had a girlfriend I was in grade seven and eight. She was the first girlfriend I really truly loved or felt I loved. Now I know she was a dysfunctional person too, with her own set of demons. I didn't know that at the time. We were too young to know anything but as I've grown I've looked back and seen that. My next girlfriend had a boyfriend. She went to another school and she just wanted to use me. This went on for about a year. This was at about the age of sixteen. From the ages of thirteen to seventeen I had my first girlfriends who I thought I had fell in love with. They kind of chewed me up and spit me out.

  By the time I had gotten a real girlfriend, an actual relationship, I had so many bad habits. I so easily went to being sexually promiscuous and being with multiple partners behind my girlfriend's back. I didn't do it to hurt her because I truly loved her. Here was somebody that I loved very much and had incredibly strong feelings for. She was just a beautiful person in my life. There were a lot of beautiful moments and experiences we shared throughout that relationship. But, I was this dysfunctional person, a very hurting and confused person. I only knew how to get gratification and a sense of self worth through sex. It was with her that I first became abusive with women. During the course of our relationship there were seven to ten times when things really got out of hand. The abuse at those times was at all levels - physical, mental, emotional and spiritual. I really hurt her and to this day I'm sorry that I did that. I wish I could have spared her that anguish and hurt because I truly loved her.

  I never gave myself time to grieve that relationship before I got into a new one. So, I carried all of my dysfunction plus my relationship issues into my most recent relationship. There was a lot of good in this relationship. The greatest gifts I received from that were my children. Yet our differences and our individual issues were just too much for us to get through.

  I didn't want a dysfunctional lifestyle anymore but I didn't know where to turn to get help for myself. I was scared to reach out to someone and admit I was all messed up. I didn't want to hurt anybody anymore. I wanted to be happy. I knew cheating and being promiscuous was wrong and it wasn't going to bring me my happiness. Drinking wasn't helping either. It wasn't doing me any favours. My drinking resulted in a lot of negative consequences, hurt and pain. Over time the seed of change was planted but it took a long time to grow. It took a long time to get to the point where I said, "I don't want this anymore. I've had enough negative living. I want to start to live life." I started my healing journey and I'm incredibly grateful for that. I just wish I could have come to that point a lot sooner in life. But, I know the hardships and the suffering I've had to experience have helped me to make up my mind that I want a better life for myself.

With help I was able to turn all of the negatives into positives by learning and growing from it. It has helped me in becoming my true self, who I truly am. I've just started that journey. In sobriety, I am able to return to our culture, our way, and return to our ceremonies. I am able to learn with a clear mind. I am learning to love myself and take those necessary positive steps in the right direction onto a good path. It is still a real struggle for me to always use a good mind but it's a struggle I welcome.

The real turning point for me was when I physically assaulted my ex-girlfriend. It happened when we were out at a bar and the cops were called. I went to jail and I got out but I was charged. I was incredibly sorry that I had hurt her, that I had hit her. It was the first time I really, really hurt her. I was extremely drunk, not to say that's an excuse, but I lost control and I know I could have really seriously injured her. She could have ended up in the hospital or worse. Throughout our relationship I abused her in many ways but up until that time this event was by far the worst. I loved this woman and I didn't want to hurt her so while I was in jail I decided that was it. I said to myself, "This is it. You need to get help. This is enough. This woman is a beautiful woman. She's got a good heart. She's stuck by you. You've done so much to her. You owe it to her and to yourself. You owe it to our children to get help, to end this stupid, vicious cycle of dysfunction." So I requested to get help, to go into treatment. I knew the courts would go along with it. This was my opportunity for change. One of my probation orders was that I seek counselling for alcohol and anger-management. It was really specified that I seek counselling for my problem with alcohol.

I thought of either going to Ganohkwásra⁷ or a treatment centre. I was still kind of scared. I knew Ganohkwásra⁷ was a safe place. By this time the stigma of the battered woman shelter, or the "she didn't listen shelter," was kind of gone. People were seeing that it was a positive thing. It was really becoming a great, beautiful healing place and a respected place. I knew, deep down, it was going to be a healthy place for me. Yet a part of me wasn't certain. I was tremendously scared but that's how I came to Ganohkwásra⁷.

My experience at Ganohkwásra⁷ has been one of great joy. The decision to follow through with this, to help myself, to heal, to be committed to this, was the greatest decision of my life. I am so grateful for all the many beautiful, caring, helping, healing people who work there. Ganohkwásra⁷ has been a saviour for me in many ways. It has helped me give myself my rebirth to our culture and our ways. Ganohkwásra⁷ has such a holistic approach. They combine the cultural aspect with the healing and the rational thinking.

The people of Ganohkwásra⁷, my counsellor and everybody there, have been so wonderful. They always greet me with a comfortable smile. I never feel judged. They are happy to see that I am another Onkwehonwe man in healing or looking for help. They are happy to help me in whatever way they can, whether it is through kind words or support or teaching me new ways to look at things, healthier behaviour, or a healthier mindset, or just giving a friendly smile, saying hello or greeting me at the door. It's just an incredibly beautiful place that I am tremendously grateful for. I can't say enough about it.

Ganohkwásra⁷ has also helped me to see and appreciate the tremendous help and support I was getting from my family. That support has a lot more meaning to me now. I can appreciate the love I receive from my family, my parents and loved-ones.

In a lot of my initial sessions my counsellor urged me and showed me how easy it was to get back, to break down the barriers of being too scared to know my culture. I had wanted that for a long time in my life and was slowly working to that point. Ganǫhkwásra' helped accelerate that whole process for me and break down some mental barriers I had in that regard. They showed me I didn't have to be so scared. I didn't have to be so cautious or feel silly because I didn't know my language or culture. I didn't know how to be a part of the traditional community or how to live that way.

I'm so grateful for being able to return to our culture because for so long in my childhood I can remember wanting to be a true Onkwehonwe. To me that means knowing my language, our history, our teachings, our creation story, the ceremonies, the songs, the Great Law, the Tree of Peace, the Confederacy, the wampums, the stories behind everything, using a good mind, respect and knowledge of creation, our traditional games like lacrosse and snowsnake, and just being a part of all of that. I knew I wanted that in my life. I didn't know anything about what I wanted but I knew I wanted that.

My fear prevented me from taking the steps to return to our culture. Ganǫhkwásra' has probably been the greatest help in that area for me. They have helped me take that step, given me the encouragement, given me a sense of support or security to know I'm doing what is right for me. I've learned I should go for it and I won't be dissatisfied or unhappy that I took a chance. That's exactly what happened and I am so incredibly grateful.

I've cried so many tears of joy and happiness since I've been able to return to our way to learn about our culture, to learn about our ceremonies and take part, to be able to return to the longhouse, to learn the teachings. Participating in all of that has been one of the greatest things for me. I believe participating in that way of life is just as important as knowing our ways. That's where I get a lot of satisfaction. Using a good mind is something I have to do to participate in those ceremonies. I've learned participation can mean simply being there and contributing to the longhouse, to the ceremonies, giving back to our people and sharing with them. I understand our people were very communal because we were maternally based. The women were held in great regard and respected. I believe that had a tremendous effect on us being a communal society. We were hunters but we were farmers first. We harvested the corn, beans and squash. We worked the ground and everybody depended on everybody for the good of the people. Everyone participated. Everyone had their special part to do.

The first time I went to a ceremony and was able to participate and take some food was a great experience for me. No one suggested I take food and nobody told me I had to do it. People said, "You can bring it if you want to." They basically did it in such a good way that they made it my choice. I didn't feel any pressure at all. It was something I wanted to do because that was part of participating. To give back, to share, and to allow myself to be grateful and thankful was a tremendous healing for me. The first few ceremonies I went to I didn't know enough to take any food. I took the food for granted. I was amazed at all of the food that was out. I thought, "Wow, where does all of this come from?" To see it, I knew it had come from somewhere but I didn't know everyone had taken it there. So, the first few ceremonies I went to I didn't take anything which was fine and I don't feel bad for that. I didn't know and it was a process of learning for me. But the first time I took food I was incredibly grateful and every time I go now I try to do that little bit to acknowledge not only Sonkwaya'tihson but all of creation and all of my brothers and sisters because I want to give that back. It's incredibly beautiful to give back in that way. It's very heart-warming for me to participate. I'm very grateful for that.

In my counselling I've learned about how to use a good mind and to try to apply that to every aspect of my life. I've learned I'm only going to get out of life what I put into it. For so long, I did nothing. I didn't put anything into it. I worked so hard at denying that or refusing to look at that. There was no way I was going to sell myself short. I had experienced enough pain and was fully committed to myself and getting away from the pain. I didn't want it in my life anymore. I had carried it around with me long enough. Prior to that I didn't know I had the power to change, that the power could come from within myself. With help I was able to tap into my inner strength to create the positive changes I needed.

The biggest thing that helped me within my counselling was getting over my fear of judgment. That only came with time and establishing trust and a relationship with my counsellor but it was also my commitment to my healing. I was honest and open. I was very truthful and forthright in talking about my life and my problems. I felt such relief from that burden, to get the weight off my shoulders. To talk had such a healing effect. It was good for me to get everything out, to give it its voice and its energy, to give it its life, instead of refusing it or denying it or pretending it wasn't there.

I've learned about talking about my feelings, identifying what the feelings are and where they come from. I've learned my feelings are okay and it is normal to have feelings of fear, anger, hurt, and resentment and to have questions and to not know the answers. The trust I have in **Ganohkwásra**[7], in my counsellor and in myself, allows me to be my true self. I am able to let somebody finally see the real me, to let myself out, and to let everybody see what is really, truly in my heart and in my mind. I can let people see I am a good person with a good mind and a good heart with love for myself, my family, our people, our ways and creation. I am realizing that I am becoming who I am truly meant to be. For so long I have been a distorted version of myself. Only in bits and pieces and instances have I really been my true self. I felt like I was walking through life in a fog. I wasn't able to be who I truly am. The more confidence I have in who I am, the more I can be myself. I can believe I am a good person and I can get past the things I have done in my life. As unfortunate as my experiences were to me, they didn't make me a bad person and I can still be my true self. I can still find myself and the spirituality in our culture and be able to connect. Somebody taught me that and helped me to see that gift. They helped me to see it was right there for me for my taking. All I have to do is participate and take action. It is really that simple and that helped me tremendously.

I think a real turning point in my therapy was choosing to stop drinking. Before that decision was made alcohol was one of my best friends. There were times when I would almost cradle that beer bottle in my hands. It was so precious to me. I could just lose myself in my drinking. It was an ideal atmosphere for me to get away from anything that was going in my life at the time that I didn't want to address. It was my escape. I used alcohol to torture myself too. There were times when I wondered what it would take to drink myself to death.

I had been in counselling for months before I quit drinking. One of the reasons I went to Ganǫhkwásra' was because I knew in order to get counselling there I couldn't continue to drink. At the time I knew I wanted to quit drinking but I knew I wasn't ready to just stop at that moment. I was able to wean myself. Then, that's when I really made a commitment to be sober, to put alcohol down for love of myself, for love of my children and my family and for my belief in our ways, for Sonkwaya'tihson and what he has given me. It sounds simple but the alcohol really affected me that way.

At Ganǫhkwásra' I learned about alcohol and how it's not ours. It was never meant to be ours. When I heard someone actually say, "Alcohol is not ours," it really hit me. Alcohol has brought so much pain to our people. It is an awful, vicious, horrible life. That helped me to realize and see how no good has come of alcohol. In my own life there has been no good that has come from my alcohol use and abuse. I had many laughs with friends at parties but usually it ended up with negative consequences; a hangover, doing something wrong, being with someone that I hadn't really wanted to be with, getting in a fight, embarrassing myself, embarrassing my family, or embarrassing my girlfriend. It really didn't do any good for me. Up to that point the dysfunctional behaviour, the dysfunctional thinking, and the alcohol were all a tremendously huge part of my life. It was incredible for me to be able to let it go and to see beyond that. There was a time I didn't think I could see that. I didn't think I could live to be thirty or thirty-five years old because I didn't think I could get away from alcohol. Many times I didn't want to put the alcohol down. I have had three setbacks or instances where I've relapsed. Each of those times only lasted a few hours but they helped me to confirm that I didn't want alcohol as part of my life anymore. I'm just so grateful that with a lot of help I was able to see that.

The other big factor that contributed to my decision to put down the alcohol was the fear that something might happen to my children as a result of my need to have alcohol in my life. It devastates me to think my children could be abused or violated because I left them with someone so I could go out and drink. Also, what if something happened to me? My children would be left without a father.

Overall, I have learned to respect myself and to not sell myself short. I have learned to respect my body and my mind and to respect the minds and bodies of others too. They deserve that just as much as I do. I think in this life we have all we need to survive and live the life that was given to us. It's in our teachings. It's in the Great Law. Everything we need is here in creation and it's all really quite simple. Peace and balance and serenity can be really very easy and attainable. Life can be as simple or as complicated as we make it. I guess what has really helped me a lot is to live according to my heart and what is in my heart because I have so much beauty and love in my heart. I firmly believe if you follow your heart you can't go wrong. If you listen to your heart and use a good mind, life is very beautiful and simple. It can be very fulfilling very easily and that is so comforting to know.

I guess that's what I'm striving for now, to have balance everyday. Today I know when I don't have that balance I have the tools and the resources to help me to find it again. I have the ability to work through it myself or I have many resource people to help me and different places I can turn to. Living a good life helps that process along. I know when I am living true to my heart with a good mind and a good heart I'm not doing much I would regret. I'm not saying things or behaving in a way that is negative or harmful to other people. I believe there are less things to regret or less that I have to worry about.

For me, there's beauty, simplicity and humility in knowing that I'm part of something, that I'm here for a reason and that I matter in life, in creation. It is such a beautiful gift to see, feel, live and contribute to the beauty of creation. It's amazing, simply amazing. Sonkwaya'tihson has blessed me with so much in my life. I wouldn't say it's our obligation to live a good life but I guess if we learn in a good way then it's like you can't help but give back, to want to show your gratefulness. I know I do.

To wrap up my personal story of sexual abuse and healing I would like to say that sexual abuse can have a devastating effect on our lives. Nobody deserves to be subjected to that. When we come into this world we're a gift, as children we're the greatest gift. Children are so full of innocence and life. They don't deserve sexual abuse. We should do whatever we can to protect them and show them respect. No one deserves to be sexually assaulted or abused, especially not children. Our bodies are our own. They're our special bodies. Everybody is special and we all have the right to the security of our bodies, that they won't be violated or taken advantage of.

In the last year or so I have learned so much and I have changed almost everything about my life. It hasn't been a total makeover but in many ways I am a different person. I'd like to say I'm blossoming and transforming into my true self and I'm better able to share that with everybody. Life is too precious. It's so short. It's too beautiful to waste on negativity or painful things. We get one chance, one time through life. Make the best of it. Look at the beauty in the sky, the water, the trees, the flowers, the children, your family and your loved ones. I hope to live the rest of my life like that. When it's all done and over with I want to be able to say I've lived a good life and I don't regret anything. The first part of my life wasn't as good as it could have been but there was a lot of good in what I learned in those years to make the next years of my life that much more meaningful and enjoyable. I'm doing just that.

Looking Glass

I lay awake, and I wonder aloud,
"Where do I go, what do I do now?"
Then inside, a voice thunders deep,
"Be quiet, just go back to sleep!

Why are you so mean?
What did I do?
Why don't you love me?
I've always loved you.

This image I have of that little boy,
Crying and crying, but never heard,
He raises his hand to wipe away the mist,
The mist that covers the image,
Looking back from the glass.

Who is that looking back,
With such a sadness in his eyes?
Why is there no one to hear him,
Or hold him close when he cries?

Where does he go,
When the lights are turned out?
He just goes back,
Back inside where he can't hear the shouts.

Maybe some day,
When the tears have all dried,
He'll awake and wonder
Without tears in his eyes.
Where do I go, what will I do?
Can you help me decide, Dad?
I still love you …

R. LaForme

Journal

Journaling is a great way to express our thoughts and feelings. It is a safe way for us to "talk it out," at times resulting in our awareness of solutions and connections we were previously unaware of. This form of "venting" also allows us to get our thoughts and feelings outside of ourselves. Holding them in will often cause us further distress so getting it out on paper is a form of healthy release.

You may begin your journaling by writing down everything you are thinking and feeling. At first, it may take you a long time to do your journaling because you have so many thoughts and feelings racing through you, just waiting to get out. Just allow yourself to write down whatever comes to you. Later your journaling can become more focused and purposeful.

If your are experiencing difficulties while reading the stories within this book try writing a letter to the Creator, a parent, or someone else you feel safe with. You may also direct the letter to the child part of yourself. If you have been sexually abused and this is why you are experiencing difficulties, we do not recommend writing a letter to the perpetrator. Without the assistance of a counsellor or therapist, this could do more harm than good for you.

Keep your journal in a safe place. If this cannot be done, destroy or burn your journal afterwards. When you burn it, the smoke will take your words to the Creator where they will be safe.

"It wasn't always my fault"

"It wasn't always my fault."

I don't know where to begin because I've worked on a lot of sexual abuse since I have been going to Ganǫhkwásra'. It was hard growing up not being believed, not being heard or acknowledged. Going to Ganǫhkwásra', for once in my life someone heard me, someone believed me, someone listened and someone cared. My counsellor was so very genuine. She was also Haudenosaunee, Onkwehonwe and that made a very big difference. It has been so nice to be able to talk about anything and everything, especially our traditional beliefs, and she would understand. I can't remember or count the number of times I was sexually abused. When I last counted there was about fourteen different people in my life I was sexually abused by, male and female, always family members.

My first memory of being sexually abused was when I was eight years old. I was walking home from school with my brothers and an older boy. This older boy dragged me into the ditch where he sexually abused me. My brothers laughed and left me there. When I went home my mother didn't believe me. She yelled at me, telling me it was my fault, that I shouldn't have been walking behind them. She examined me in front of my brothers. I had such shame and disgust of my body which affected the rest of my life. The police didn't believe me. The doctor who examined me said there was no sign of a struggle since my clothes weren't torn. Nobody believed me or cared. It was my fault. I shouldn't have been doing this or that.

I grew up thinking everything was always my fault, hating and doubting my own reality, at times thinking I was crazy. My mother told everyone I was crazy when I tried to speak my truth and my reality. I wasn't comfortable being in the same room with people who abused me. I couldn't stand them looking at me. I just had so much disgust. After a while I quit trying to tell my mother about anything because she didn't believe me, or she would say it was my fault anyway.

I was sexually abused by both of my parents too. There was only one time by my parents but one time was one too many times. I wasn't safe anywhere. I realize I have difficulty forming friendships as I had learned not to trust women. This is an issue I continue to work on.

I had a lot of anger and resentment towards my mother, for not listening, not caring, not protecting me and not believing me. She never did believe me. She blamed me. She always told me it was my fault. If anyone sexually abused me it was always my fault. They didn't do anything wrong. When I was young I kept a journal and I wrote about all of the things that were happening. My mom found it once and read it. She said, "You're crazy, these things didn't happen." She showed it to all of my brothers and they all laughed. She said, "See, I told you she's crazy." I always felt so alone. I felt like I didn't have a mother. She was never there.

There were a lot of times I hated her so much that when I spoke to her I wanted to slap her. When I left home for good it was because she kicked me out. There was an incident with other family members that she blamed me for. It had nothing to do with me but she blamed me anyway. She told me, "It's all your damn fault!" I remember her standing there and stomping her feet as she yelled at me. I said, "Oh, you act so childish." That was it. She said, "Get the hell out!" So I left. I didn't have to be told twice. I left and I never went back.

Things carried on this way right into my adulthood. I would call her or go to her house at times but it was never a regular thing. When I did go there she was always putting me down. She never acknowledged me, hardly talked to me. When she did, it was always negative.

When my son was born she didn't want to see him. When she did see him she said, "Look at his funny shaped head." She didn't have anything nice to say about him. The next day my brother had a son. She went to see him and she said, "Oh look, I finally got a grandson with black hair." He was so great and my son was less. My son had black hair and he still does.

I had married a man that was just as abusive to me as my mother was. He abused me physically, verbally, mentally, emotionally and sexually. To me, it feels like I let him. I thought it was okay because whatever happened was always my fault anyway. I deserved it. I didn't have any self-esteem or self-confidence. I stayed in that marriage because I was told, "You made your bed, now lie in it." In those days people were expected to stay married, no matter what.

I went back to school after I had been married for fifteen years. I had quit school at a rather young age because I felt I needed to contribute to looking after my younger brothers and sisters. I would buy them school clothes because I was almost like their mother. I was the oldest girl in my family so I was a caretaker from a very early age. There was never time for me. An aunt of mine, who passed away recently, was a role model for me. She was a nurse and I had always wanted to be a nurse so I took a Health Care Aid course. I worked really hard but I wanted to quit. I believed I couldn't succeed, that I wasn't good enough. My husband only reinforced this with his own insecurities. He would say, "Who do you think you are? You think you're so good. What do you want to do that for?" Those are the exact words my mother would say to me. My husband didn't want me to finish school because he knew I would eventually have what I needed to be independent from him. I stayed with him for seventeen years. He called me down and put my children down. I took it all.

When I went back to school my teacher believed in me. She supported me and said, "I'm not going to let you quit." She really believed in me and I won a merit award when I graduated from that course even though I had a difficult time believing in myself. She sent me to this home for the aged and handicapped. When I went there they said, "You know, you come highly recommended." I was shocked and overwhelmed. I was treated very well there. I did my job and did the best I could. They thought quite highly of me and I was able to gain some self-respect and confidence. So, after two years, I finally left my husband. I had a good paying job to support my children without him.

The night I left him, he had gotten home drunk and started choking me. I went into my son's bedroom and discovered he was sleeping with a knife underneath his pillow. My husband came into the bedroom after he had been choking me and he passed out on the floor. I thought, "I should get back at him, make him pay for everything he did to us." That's when I realized what I was putting my children through and that someone was going to get seriously hurt, someone was going to die.

I couldn't take it anymore regardless of how many times he called saying he was sorry and it wouldn't happen again, he'd never hurt me again. He threatened to kill himself as he had done several times before. I told him to go ahead and do it because I knew he wouldn't. I waited seventeen years and still he didn't change. I never went back. He cried but I knew it was just the same cycle that had been repeated throughout our marriage. He would hurt us then make all of these promises and never follow through. It just repeated over and over again.

I went through so much with my son after that. He blamed me because his father had told him I was a slut and a whore and that I was running around with all of these different men. I said, "Gee, where are they?" How could I have different men when I hated myself and hated my body?

I continued to stay a victim my whole life, letting people take advantage of me, getting into abusive, unhealthy relationships. I believed I didn't deserve anything better. I wasn't important. I didn't matter. I was ugly. I was dumb. I was good for nothing. Who the hell would want me anyway? Those were the beliefs I had about myself.

Eventually, I got sick and tired of being a victim. I got sick and tired of being abused. There have been people in my life who believed in me and I was beginning to believe in myself.

I began to see a non-Native counsellor and, together with a doctor, it was decided I needed to be on anti-depressants because I had an eating disorder. I had bulimia for many years. I stayed on this medication for a long time, numbing myself. When I began to see my counsellor at Ganǫhkwásra' I weaned myself off the medication. That was one of my goals in counselling. I said, "I don't want to be on these anymore. I want to feel. For once in my life I want to feel what's there. I want to be able to feel, I want to be real, I want to be human, I want to be me."

I remember the first time I went to see my counsellor. The one question she asked me that really threw me was, "How did you get from there to where you are now?" I just looked at her and I said, "I never really thought about it." To say the skills and techniques of my counsellor were good would be an understatement. I am so thankful for all she has done for me. A lot of the work I did with her involved different techniques such as EFT (tapping), psychodrama, release work, art therapy and EMDR (Eye Movement Desensitization and Reprocessing).[*] I certainly benefited from all, but I believe EMDR was what really helped me change the beliefs I had about myself.

    For me, EMDR sessions were about repairing those negative beliefs I had about myself. I had a lot of EMDR sessions because there were a lot of incidents I needed to work on. I started with the beliefs that I couldn't do anything right, I was no good, and I couldn't have an opinion. My counsellor would help me to go back to an incident in my mind. I would talk about what happened then I would talk about what I was feeling at that time. Then, we would look at what is happening now and how I was feeling. Finally, we would go back to the original incident and I would change it. It was really working on a spiritual level. I would ask for my helpers to come and I would do what I needed to change the message and create a positive belief. In the end, I had different beliefs. Now I know that I can do anything I set my mind to, I am important and my opinions matter.

    Another thing that has really changed within me is my anger. I had a lot of anger, resentment and jealousy and rightly so. I had been abused by so many people and I believed I deserved everything that happened to me because it was all my fault. That's the belief I had about myself growing up and throughout my life. I couldn't make decisions, I didn't have a voice and I couldn't get angry because I was so scared of it. To me anger was violence. Growing up, my mom and dad were very violent, as was my ex-husband.

    I think I realized after both my parents passed away that I had a lot of fear of them when they were alive. So now I believe I'm allowed to feel my anger and it's alright for me to be angry and I don't have to be afraid anymore. I hadn't realized the depth of my fear and anger. More and more it's coming out that I do have a lot of fear. I grew up in fear of a lot of people in my family, especially my own parents.

---

[*] For a brief description of these therapeutic techniques please refer to p. 204 &205.

With the help of **Ganǫhkwásra'** I was able to feel and get to my anger. I remember when I first started I couldn't swear and I let people walk all over me. I would just smile. I now realize it's safe for me to express my feelings. Doing the release work along with a psychodrama about my mother, really helped me work through that.

I have also taken training in psychodramatic bodywork. I went back to school again in a Social Service Worker program and this training has helped me both personally and professionally. At first, I couldn't get to my anger because I had a lot of fear of going into it. I would want to just break down and cry. I'd want to just collapse and cry because that was my way. Now, I know doing that work and staying with my anger is staying with my own power. By staying with my own power I am staying with my strong identity. Now, I can do my anger work and cry too because I am able to stay with my anger and speak in a clear voice.

I understand now that I had become like my mother, someone I didn't want to be like. I always said I would never be like her and as much as I fought that I recognize I did become like her. My mom died with a lot of sadness because she didn't work on these things. She died letting people walk all over her and take advantage of her. She died being a victim. That was what she chose. I'm not going to be a victim anymore, I'm not going to let everyone walk all over me. I'm not going to be taken advantage of anymore. And, all the anger I had toward my mother is gone. I worked on so many things that when my mom was sick and dying, I was able to nurture her, love her and care for her. I was able to give her everything she didn't give me because she couldn't. I don't resent her or hate her for that. I feel sorry for her, the way she had to live, the way she chose to live. I really feel sorry that she let herself live that way.

Now, I'm just doing the very best I can and I know I miss my mom. The regret I do have is that I didn't work on myself sooner so we could've had a close relationship before she died. I wish she could have been there for me. I wish she could've said, "You have beautiful kids." I wish she could've said, "You're a good mother. You're a good daughter." There are a lot of things

I wish she could've said but she didn't. Now she's gone and she never did say them.

I have learned compassion for my mother because her own mother didn't want her. She was sexually abused by her stepfather and her mother didn't believe her. I think losing your parents is very traumatic, no matter how old you are or how difficult your relationship has been.

Being a grandparent has really made a lot of difference in my life. I'm a grandmother now and I have all of these little kids looking to me for unconditional love, guidance and direction. I will be there for them. I'm not going to be gone like my mom and dad were. That's my main focus right now, my children and my grandchildren. I watched a legacy cycle being handed down from my grandparents to my own parents, to me, to my children, to my grandchildren. I'm going to change that. I've already repeated a lot of my parents' mistakes but I'm not going to repeat the mistakes they made as grandparents. They weren't there for my kids and my kids really needed them growing up.

My daughter is going through some rough times with her daughter, my grand-daughter. My grand-daughter is feeling rejected and abandoned by an absent father. She's blaming her mother and getting angry with her because it feels safe for her to direct her anger there. I am there to mediate and listen to both objectively, being gentle and compassionate because I love them both. If I hadn't worked on my own issues, I wouldn't be able to give them what they need from me. I shared with my grand-daughter about the anger and resentment I had towards my own mother. I told her how blaming my mother for everything affected my whole life. I shared with her about letting this anger and resentment consume me. Because I held onto it, it spilled out into everything around me, into all of my relationships. I told her that now I have let that go and I am happier and content. I no longer feel desperate, inadequate and rejected. I let my grand-daughter know we all make mistakes but we learn from them and try not to keep repeating them. We talked about her anger and the underlying feelings which she is already aware of since she is currently in counselling herself. I love my children and grandchildren very much and I am so happy that I can be here for them.

Recently, I was working with a lady who was sixty years old and raising her grandchildren. She questioned why she was doing her healing at her age. She said, "What am I doing this for? Look at how old I am. What can I do? How can I help anybody now?" I went to her and very gently told her, "You know what? By helping yourself, you're helping your children and your grandchildren and that's your family. By helping yourself as an individual you're helping your family and by helping your family you're helping the community. It doesn't end right here with you." She just looked at me and said, "Thank you." I know that by helping myself I am able to prove it doesn't just stop here with me. I've learned that you can do anything you want to do, anything you try to do.

I now have a voice and an opinion. I used to cry in the past when I had difficulties with co-workers and family members. I would just go along with everyone, letting them have their way as long as nobody got angry with me. It didn't matter how I felt. I had such a fear of abandonment, rejection and anger. Now I can say, "I have an opinion too." Sometimes they don't like my opinion, but that's alright, they don't have to. I have an opinion and they have theirs. I have to think about myself. I am important. I think people have been shocked by this "new me." I'm still working on my boundaries and setting my limitations. I know how to say no now which wasn't a part of my vocabulary before. It's alright if someone gets angry with me, they'll get over it. If they don't, that's their problem.

There's so much to life and mine has only begun. I don't regret all my life experiences I've had. My parents did the best they could with the tools they had and what they were taught from their parents. I did the best I could but I can't dwell on what was, what should've been. I can only concentrate on now. Only I and the Creator have control of what that looks like for me. I truly believe I am a strong person today because I survived all of that. I'm a strong grandmother. I'm a strong woman. I'm a strong mother. I'm a strong auntie. I am changing the legacy of abuse in my family. My son and two of my grandchildren are going for counselling. My daughter is talking about it and that's further than before and that wasn't part of the legacy!!!

This story is dedicated to **Ganǫhkwásra'** and especially my counsellor. You have helped me to realize it wasn't always my fault and I'm not crazy. You have helped me to discover myself and my gifts. I will be forever grateful.

Let's talk about the pain
No work, no gain

I go through each day
And wonder away

About what life could have been without it
Would I be normal? Could I have fit?

In this world of prejudice and ridicule
To be rough and tough is the only rule

I know I'm different, I will not fight
I feel so worthless some cold nights

I began to talk and understand
I am a good person with lots at hand

I am strong and handsome and have many gifts to share
So get to know me, you'll see if you dare

I have been through things you couldn't imagine
Wouldn't change a thing, and I won't like it again

Experience has made me who I am today
Kind and gentle and funny I'd say

I didn't ask to be this way
Understand, that's all I'd have to say

Yes I am different in many ways
If we were all the same, I'd be you today!

Anonymous

Pray or meditate.

Talk to the Creator. Our teachings tell us we are never alone. We each carry a part of the Creator with us and therefore the Creator is always with us. If these stories are emotionally upsetting and take you back to memories of past traumas, pray for guidance and talk to the Creator about your thoughts and feelings. Answers may not come to you directly; however, in time, they will most likely appear when you least expect them.

Meditation is an exercise in quieting or calming our minds. Its main purpose is to assist us in becoming more connected with our inner self, our true self. If you are becoming overwhelmed by the feelings you are experiencing while reading this book, meditation can help to calm you. It can bringing your attention back to your centre therefore helping you to ground yourself again (grounding – quieting the mind, settling your feelings and being in the present). There are many types of meditation to learn and all of them have proven beneficial. For beginners, try the following guidelines:

1. Find a quiet place.
2. Relax your body, quiet your mind.
3. Breathe deeply, concentrating on the inhaling and exhaling of your breath.
4. Let go of your worries and cares.
5. Feel the presence of peace within you.
6. If you begin to feel your attention and thoughts drifting, concentrate on your breathing again and bring yourself back to your inner peace.
7. Don't worry about doing it right and don't have expectations of seeing things or experiencing some sort of revelation. Being able to quiet our minds has its own benefits. Answers from within will come eventually as you connect with your inner self and your higher power.
8. Remember, staying focused comes easier with time and practice.

"I just wanted to be loved"

"I just wanted to be loved."

Today I am an adult, but I still have an inner child alive and well. I first became self-aware when I was approximately a year old. That is just a guess. I do remember being too young to get up and walk. It was a struggle for me to just roll over. I remember I would snuggle close to my father, in reality I am just guessing that it was my father; I have no recollection of my mother. I remember waking up in the morning; it was cold in the house. My father and I were sleeping on the floor upstairs. I was reaching out, the way infants do, trying to touch the white rabbits, they were hopping around on the floor while I lay watching. I was cold, but still I kept reaching for the rabbits. My hands were repeatedly opening and closing, but I could not grasp those beautiful white balls of fur.

My next clear memory, I would guess to be about the age of two years old. I am standing in the kitchen by the table and a chair. My father is stacking books on the chair for me to sit on so I could eat my breakfast. Yet, I don't know what time it was, it could have been dinnertime. Today, right now, I can still hear my father's words, "Eat your cornflakes, that's all we got." I remember sitting on top of all those books, looking down at the floor, hoping I wouldn't fall. Sitting there straight and tall, with my chin still below the surface of the table, I ate all my cornflakes.

I stayed in a lot of different places with a lot of people. I know this because when I meet people and they find out who I am, they say, "Oh yeah, I used to look after you." To this day, I have found no reason to disbelieve anyone.

When I was approximately twenty-eight to thirty inches tall, on a cold, dark and rainy night, my father took me to live with some people. My father carried me in the house and stood me on the floor. He just left me there with these strange people. The women of the house gave me rice with raisins. When I went to sleep that night, my bed was on two kitchen chairs, side by side, shoved up against the wall, so that when I laid down, the wall as on one side and the backs of the chairs on my other side. My head was not hanging over and neither were my feet. My thoughts of falling off my bed left me when I had seen that it was long enough. Right now, I still remember that night, I didn't sleep very much. Sleeping across two chairs was a new experience for me.

I spent four or five years with this family after my father left me there. During this time, I learned how to hate, I learned to take beatings and not complain. I learned to take abuse from the other children and never utter a word. I learned how to fight for my life, my very existence, at the tender age of about five years. I learned how to get drunk at age six years because I didn't care. I learned how to feel happy inside of me when my peers suffered a physical injury. That was my successful way of fighting back. When I had seen one of my foster brothers break an arm, it was the first time in my life that I experienced happiness and joy inside of me.

I learned how to want for a mother and father. I learned not to trust anyone. I learned how it feels to be struck by a vicious blow of an adult's hand and land across the room, all for seeking nurturance from an adult. I learned the pain of being told, "Don't act like that, you are not my kid." I learned the terror of being repeatedly suffocated to unconsciousness. I learned to block out being sexually abused, only to have the nightmares come back thirty years later and cause me extreme pain and suffering, which I did in silence. I learned to keep my pain inside and not let anyone see it, because if they saw my pain, they would inflict more pain upon me. I learned how to stay out of people's way and ran most of my whole life.

When I was seven years old, someone, I don't know who, took me to the States. They left me there with total strangers. One of those strangers was my father. The other adult stranger was his wife, my stepmother. I was there for two years. Today, I really believe my stepmother used me as a stand-in for my absent father. She used to beat the living shit out of me. I would try and figure out why she beat me and not her children. I can remember thinking I didn't do it, it was her own daughter who had done whatever it was I got a beating for. It didn't do me any good to tell the truth because she wouldn't believe me.

My dad was always drunk when he came home. Well, actually he didn't come home, his wife would always go out, find him and drag him home. Then they took turns beating each other.

One or the other always had a black eye or eyes, or big bruises.

When they would fight there were no rules. Sometimes she would have to put more clothes on. Then she would go right back, kicking, swinging, biting, scratching, frying pans, bats, in the mud, blood and the beer. They would wreck the furniture, turn over the stove, break the windows, and rip off the doors. The other children and I would lie on the floor peeking down stairs watching the fight. One time when they were fighting, she got a hold of a 12 gage shotgun. She had it loaded beforehand. My daddy ran and when he went out the door he slammed it behind himself. She fired that shotgun through the wall about 12 or 15 inches from the edge of the door. She put a hole clear through the wall to the outside. She missed him because he jumped in the opposite direction. He was on the other side of the house looking in the window until she got that gun re-loaded. My dad was kind of scarce around there for a while after that.

I was able to get out of there when I was nine years old. My dad's brother and his wife were visiting. I had never seen or heard of them before that day I turned nine. I just came right out and asked them if I could live with them. They said no, so I cried really hard and lots, because even at nine years old I figured one day my stepmother was going to beat me to death. I could not tell my dad what she was doing to me because she would beat me more for telling him. I know that for a fact because I told on her just once and sure enough, she beat me the very next time he was gone. Damn, I sure didn't do that again.

My adopted father (uncle) was stationed at an Air Force base when I went to live with him and his wife. This was a big turning point in my life. Not too long after I went to live with my aunt and uncle, my uncle gave me a whipping with a belt because I stole a toy from the store. I sure didn't steal anything after that; not toys anyway.

I used to steal food and hide it all over the house, any place I thought no one could find it. Well, I had so many caches of food all over the house, I guess a blind man could have found most of it. They did not beat me for stealing food. They just explained there was lots of food, and I could have it any time I wanted. I didn't really believe them, but I put the food back because I had gotten caught stealing it. I was expecting to get a severe beating, but it never came about. It must have been about three years before I really believed that what they said about the food was true. There was always lots, and it was always there. Every night until I was twelve years old from when I was nine, I would get up in the middle of the night, sometimes two or three times. I would go to the kitchen and look at the food, just to make sure it was still there. It took me three years to believe my aunt and uncle that there was lots of food and it would always be there.

 My uncle and his wife became my legally adoptive parents in 1962, when I turned 12 years old. By that time, I had settled into a trusting, loving life with them. My adopted father worked away for a year. He did it for extra money so we could move to another state. That's when my stepmother started being sexual with me. She would fix my shirt and collar every morning before I went to school, meanwhile her PJs were loose and partially unbuttoned so I could look at her breasts hanging right in front of me. She used to rub my back then she would get me to rub her back while she was naked.

 One time when we were on the beach this guy was trying to pick up my mother. I knew what he was trying to do. From what I understood or believed, it was him, not my mother. Boy was I stupid. Anyway, before we departed in our separate vehicles, after my mother was in the car, I was scared but I walked up to that man, I looked him in the eyes and I said, "My mother is a married woman, you stay away from her!" I was expecting him to beat me up before I got away from him. After I said that, I just turned around and walked away. I got into the car on the passenger side. He came over and talked to my mother, but I could not hear what was said. I was expecting her to beat me when we got home. But, she didn't beat me, not what I was expecting anyway. I had already seen her 'doe' naked in previous times but this time she tried her damnedest to have sex with me. At the time I didn't know what she was trying to do. At first I thought she was trying really hard to kill me. I knew she was trying to kill me! She had her hands on the back of my head and she had my face buried in between her bare breasts and I could not get away. I was scared and could not get away, I could not breathe, I wasn't getting any air in my nose or mouth. She was trying to kill me because I told that guy to stay away from her. She kept trying to make my penis big and hard but I didn't know what she was doing. I was just scared of the woman I had learned to love and trust. She was unsuccessful that night, when I was twelve years old.

By the time I was thirteen she had me well trained as her sex machine. Every time we had sex, I felt inside of me that something was wrong. But, I didn't want to let go of the good feeling I got every time I climaxed and the pleasure I felt getting to the climax. She would tell me, "Ram it in there!" over and over. So I did my best to "ram it in there." After I climaxed I would feel guilty, deep shame, remorse, very deep remorse right from the very beginning until I ran away when I was seventeen years old.

I used to think about killing myself. Then at some point I changed and I would think about killing her. As sure as I was breathing I knew I was going to kill her. Then I thought of my adoptive father. It was going to hurt him if I killed her. So I planned my escape and when the feeling was right, I did it. I got away without being caught. By the time I ran away, I was unable to look at my adoptive mother with anything except disgust, and deep hate. Those feelings smoldered for decades. After I ran away I started to hate myself this time, almost more than I hated her.

To compensate for the sexual abuse, I started to get into sports which is how I got rid of the anger and frustration. I would run for hours, non-stop, through the bushes. If I didn't run, surely as I am here today, I would have taken my adoptive mother's life. When I was eighteen, I was trying to be responsible for myself but the anger and frustration were still there. To alleviate it, I started working ten to eighteen hours a day, five to seven days a week and sometimes longer. When I finished working, I would lay down and go right to sleep in less than a minute.

From the age of 18 years to 28 years, I functioned in a very self-destructive manner. I took risks that made my adrenaline flow, mostly because it would have taken the power of a hurricane to cover up the pain, anger, and torment inside of my head and my heart. I never learned to function in a healthy manner. I never learned how to look after myself properly. I always wanted or needed someone else to nurture me, love me, care for me, touch me and hold me.

After I was on my own, I didn't know how to act around girls. I was full of shame because of where I had been, and what I had experienced. I was scared of girls. I tried to be the perfect date when I would go out with a girl. I would not touch them or abuse them in any way. They would not go out with me any more after the first date.

When I was twenty I found a girl who kept going out with me even though we were not having sex. She was willing to be with me in a family way. I told her I was sexually abused by my adoptive mother. There was nothing we could do except cry. Back then there was no such thing as counsellors except in someone's mind. So my wife and I settled into a married life. Eventually, she learned to turn her back to me and not touch me. I lived a life starving for attention and affection. Whenever we had sex I was having sex with my adopted mother.

My father was an alcoholic and I didn't want to be an alcoholic so I chose to continue with my work-a-holic behaviours to deal with my pain. Life continued in this manner until I turned 28 years old. At this time, I suffered a severe industrial accident. When I think about that today, that was another turning point in my life. I was forced to lie in bed for a year. I spent much more than a year in bed, but, the extra time was self-inflicted. I tried to get "mental help" while in the hospital, but the nurses acted like they didn't care or maybe they didn't know what to do. Anyway, I got no response. I went to see doctors and was too ashamed to tell them of the abuse I had suffered growing up. Since I couldn't work out my problems physically, I was forced to think about them and relive them.

As a child I had terrorizing dreams. Every night I would try to stay awake. I didn't want to close my eyes because of the terrorizing things that were going to happen to me. Night after night, year after year, every night was the same. When I was fourteen years old I started to fight back in my dreams. I fought like a starving wolverine fighting a pack of wolves for a dead moose. Every night I beat the demons that were trying to kill me. After that I had regular nightmares that were not life threatening.

The sexual abuse I have experienced actually started when I was an infant. I have memories of choking on a penis but I was able to block and bury the conscious understanding of that until I was in my mid to late twenties. I would wake up gagging and choking and suffocating from the lack of air because in my dreams I would relive the times I had a penis in my throat. In the night, I would wake, sitting up gasping for air. My wife would wake up and ask me what was wrong. I would just say, "Nothing. I couldn't breath." I was too ashamed to tell her I was choking on a penis.

By the time I was thirty-five our oldest son was mid-teens. My wife was being a good, loving, helpful mother. Because of the things I had seen growing up, I thought she was having sex with our son. My train of thought was that if she is having sex with our son then I was going to stop it. From my experience, all the signs were there. Only one way to find out, ask! So I did. "Are you having sex with our son?" After I asked the question I found out not all mothers raise their sons in the manner which I was raised.

After months and months and years of no loving attention from my wife, starving for affection and having dreams of killing my adoptive mother and choking on a penis, I needed help. I needed a hug. I went to my sister and asked her if she could hold me, if I could give her a hug and hold her. She went to her kitchen door, looked out for about thirty seconds then turned around and came back to the kitchen chair I was sitting on. She undressed in front of me, I undressed. We lay on the kitchen floor. That was the beginning. It was some years later, during one of our talks, she shared with me that she had been sexually abused at the age of four years. Our mother knew at the time but did nothing about it. So my attempt to get help did not work. As far as my family went for help, it was the blind leading the blind.

I gave one of my other sisters a hug; the next minute we were having sex. I wanted to be touched in a loving, caring fashion, yet no one would touch me in a healthy way. I was always starving for touch. My girl cousins would come to my house and I would wind up exposing myself to them hoping they would want to touch me. Sometimes I would go to Hamilton and buy a prostitute then hate myself afterward. I never raped or assaulted anyone, though it crossed my mind. The thought of hurting someone hurt my own self, so that didn't cross my mind often. I would terminate my own life before I would hurt another human being. I lived with one woman for twenty-four years and I never struck her once, and I never threatened to strike her.

My low point in life was when all I could see in my future was my death. I wanted help for years, but I didn't know what to do, or where to go. My first wife told me she knew a woman who could help me. That is when she introduced me to a counsellor at Ganohkwásra'. I still see her today on a regular basis. On her referral, I entered into a treatment centre at forty-two years of age. Since then, my life has turned around. I am able to feel happiness and life is getting better.

My turning point in therapy was when I found out I am not to blame, I have rights, I can say "no" to whomever, whenever I want. I can say "no" and I don't have to explain. I can say "no" just because! I felt better and stronger when I swept all the old bones out of the closet. When I eliminated the secrets, the hurt, the pain, the shame and the anger, it all seems to have less effect on me. The feelings are still inside of me, but a lot less. Life is getting good. With hard work and time, I expect it to get better. I honestly don't believe I could have survived this long or made my life better without the excellent and quality help I have received from my counsellor at Ganohkwásra' and my other supports.

Today, in general my life is pretty good. Sexual abuse turned my life upside down when I was one year old. I expect my life to go on for at least another fifty years, only they will be good, happy times, honest, loving times, hard sometimes, but honest and loving. It is up to me how my life is going to be. I have learned I am not alone. People do care about others. It is that way because I care.

I have come to understand I am a spirit having a human experience. No one is to blame for the traumas in life. It's just that "shit happens." Many times our problems are handed down or given to us. Everyone is carrying their own issues and sometimes people try to hand off some of it to another person. So a lot of what we carry isn't really our own. As children, this happens most often with our parents and other significant adults in our lives. Yet, they are not to blame since a lot of what they are carrying is not their own either. It has been passed to them from someone else. We all need to do the work necessary to figure out which of the junk we carry is really our own and which is not.

In counselling, I have learned I'm not the only one this has happened to. I thought I was the only one. I was forbidden to speak about what went on at home. Now I realize many of us have been sexually abused. And, it's important to acknowledge it's not just men who abuse. Women can be perpetrators of sexual assault too. It's not just women and girls who get hurt. Men and boys get hurt too.

I have learned that sharing our trials and tribulations with others lets them know they are not alone. Sharing our injuries allows us to start new healthy habits, and a new way of living and being. It allows us to shed the shame and guilt we have carried for someone else. Shame and guilt are warning signs to us. They let us know we have strayed from our path. To carry shame and guilt only puts a cloud over our spirit, and it shades us from having sunshine in our life.

When you reach a point in your life where you think, "The only thing left for me is death," then it is time for you to seek help from our fellow spirits at **Ganǫhkwásra'**. Counselling is not a bad thing. Counselling is like getting a new start in a mature body. Still, counselling only works when we ask for it because we are tired of existing in this rut, because we want to live, we want to be more tomorrow than we are today. We have to ask for help before anyone knows we want help. I asked several times for help. At first I was asking the wrong people. I kept asking until the right person heard me. As long as we are still breathing we have the opportunity to change. Age is irrelevant. A friend of mine experienced the joy and calm of growth from counselling at **Ganǫhkwásra'** while in his seventies.

Thanks a bunch to people who care.

My Fortress

It wasn't always this way
Cast iron walls with brick mortar supports
The walls made this place largely vacant
I built many places to hide in this fortress

Before I poured the walls I was open and ready
Each raid on my soul stoked the furnace
Every attack a new tool in my growing arsenal
Pain fashioned my armour

Like any soldier, battle made me weary
I longed for peace but lost the doorway
This fortress was falling apart
And I couldn't find the way out

As the wall crumbled I turned away,
I saw deeper into the places I was protecting
Small, delicate, fragile, but brilliant and colourful
A world of life tucked away behind a bleak wall

Like the armour I wore I'd become a shell
Empty without purpose beyond survival
I forgot the spirit and soul that was present before me
This tired and brittle soldier needed more to live for than war

Before this shell crumbled like the iron walls around me
I fell into the soul that I had abandoned, yet protected
I wanted to be whole again
And found it by embracing within myself

Today, my armour is my soul
My fortress is my spirit
Love and belief are my weapons
They protect without the pain

Anonymous

Connect with creation

Open a window while you read or read outside. The air around us will hold the energy we put into it. Opening a window allows the wind to take any negative energy away. The Creator has given us the wind to help us. It is the job of the wind to clean out the negativity. When you are outside the wind will help to clear your mind. That's part of its job. Let it clean you off and carry away whatever may be bothering you.

Go for a walk outside. Let the earth take the negative energy away from your feet. The earth is our mother. She provides us with love and support. She will take our pain away from our hearts by allowing us to connect to her strength and love through our feet and throughout our whole body. She knows how to care for that energy.

As women, we can pray to the moon, our Grandmother. We have a natural connection to her as she regulates menstrual cycles as well as the conception and birth of children. Talk to her as you would your ideal Grandmother figure. Ask her to take the heaviness you are carrying; ask her for guidance; and if you feel it's necessary, ask her to help you find forgiveness within yourself.

As men, we can pray to the Sun, our Elder Brother. The sun has a special relationship with all the male species of the world. Ask him to take the heaviness you are carrying; ask him for guidance, and if you feel it's necessary, ask him to help you find forgiveness within yourself.

Hold a stone while reading the stories within this book. The stone will hold the negativity you may feel. You can keep all of the stones you have used while reading this book in a safe, closed container. When you are finished the book take the stones to the river and throw them into the river as far as you can. The water will carry the negative energy contained in the stone away from you. If you watch the rippling of the water when the stone drops into the river you will see how the rippling stops and the water settles. May this remind you of the peace you will find within once you have allowed yourself to go through a process of healing. If you don't want to wait until the end of the book, you can take each stone to the river as you have used it or find a safe place for it on the earth. The earth will know what to do with that energy just as the water does.

"I have found my voice"

"I have found my voice"

When I was little, I lived on a farm with my mother and some of my extended family. This was before televisions, DVDs and computers so most of our life revolved around activities that take place on a farm. I rarely spent a day inside. I spent most of the time outside playing on the swing, in the barns, and in the fields. I would visit the pigs, cows, horses and chickens out in the barnyard. I remember getting up early, eating, then playing in the woods all day. It was so beautiful outside. There were trees to climb, butterflies to chase, water to play in and leaves to jump in. It was an adventure every day.

My mother was very strict with me. I would get a licking when I did something wrong. I can remember how much it hurt when I got hit but I sure learned. When I was hit, it hurt and stuck in my mind. The thought of being hurt kept me from doing wrong things. Our family went to church, so we all went to church on Sundays. I would go to Sunday school with all the other kids. It seemed church people were a minority on this reserve; others went to the longhouse. I was told many times that I wasn't Indian because I went to church. I was embarrassed about going to church. I always knew that my grandmother went to longhouse at one time but gave that up, and her Clanmother duties, when she married my grandfather.

When I was little there was just my mother. I always wondered where my dad was. The only father figure I had was my grandfather. Then, while we were living with my grandparents, my mother started dating someone. I knew he wasn't my dad. I was left at home while she went out on dates. I was teased about getting a new dad. I didn't want a new dad. We were fine without someone new. Then this man started buying gifts for me. I got candy and jewellery. I had never received those things before. Looking back, I would say he was trying to buy me with gifts. It wasn't so bad. Then he and my mother got married. After that we moved to a new house on our own. It was a huge house; strange and new.

My mother and her husband both worked. One day, I came home from school and he was already there. That was the first time he touched me. I was only nine or ten years old. I was just beginning to grow breasts. He was sitting on the bed and he touched my breasts. I didn't know what was going on. I just stood there and let him touch my body. I was afraid, not knowing what was happening or why. I wanted to run away and hide but I couldn't; I froze like a deer when a spotlight is shone on it. I felt terrible and sick. I wanted to get away and wished my mother was home to help me. She always seemed to be away when this happened. I was warned by my grandmother that I should watch out what was happening but I hadn't known what she meant.

The sexual abuse carried on for many years. It didn't stop until I started dating. My mother went to work early and I would be left at home with him in the morning. I would be in bed asleep, and he would wake me up by uncovering me, touching my breasts, and touching my vagina as well as other parts of my body. I hated it. I tried to resist and was accused of being too good for him. I would get angrier and angrier. He would want to help me get dressed but I would tell him I didn't need help. I resisted as best as I could. I hated what he did to me and I wanted to leave home but where would I go? Who would believe me?

The only place I was allowed to go to visit was at my cousins' house. I even had crushes on them. They were the only guys I got to know. One of my cousins would flirt with me and he was always trying to touch my breasts. I didn't like him touching me. I liked the attention but not the fondling. One time, when we were teenagers, I went to a hotel with the two of them. They went in and I stayed in the truck. One of my cousins came back out and started to fondle me. I froze again. He lowered my pants and underwear and went down on me. Then my other cousin came out. I guess he had the same idea but when he saw that my other cousin was with me he left. I never went with them again. I loved my cousins but I didn't want to be touched by them; I didn't want to be used by them.

Because the sexual traumas I experienced began at a time when I was starting to develop my body, before getting my first moon (menstrual cycle), it changed how I would normally have felt about myself. I felt dirty. I was ashamed of my body and tried to cover it up by wearing big clothes. I began to overeat and gained a lot of weight. I had low self esteem. I began to withdraw into myself. I began to shut down my feelings and emotions to protect myself. I stopped talking to people. I talked only to myself. I also began to dissociate; my body was there but I was gone mentally. I could be asked a question, slightly hearing it and not being able to answer because it was like I wasn't there.

The first person I allowed to come into my life was my friend, then boyfriend, and then husband. He meant everything to me. I had this dream that when I got married he would be my white knight, he would take care of me and we would live happily ever after. I looked to my husband for everything. I tried to be everything for him. I waited on him and looked after him as best as I knew how. I put myself last. I didn't even know what I was all about. I was totally out of balance. There was no balance in my life.

After about two years of marriage, I wanted a child. I had always wanted children to love. I told my husband I wanted to have a baby so we began to try and after a little while, we were pregnant. I was so happy. Our baby meant so much to me. As I was growing up my family was together a lot but showed very little love and affection to one another. I don't remember ever getting a hug or a kiss so I never displayed love either. Yet, I remember saying to myself that I was going to hug and kiss my kids whenever I felt like. I wanted to show my children love. I tried to be the best mom I could be. My life revolved around my child. My husband hadn't fulfilled my needs as I had hoped, so I had this idea that my child would provide me with everything I desired. I may have even smothered her because I was so over-protective. I loved my child and wanted her to love only me, just as I had wanted from my husband. Two years went by and we had our second child. My family meant everything to me. I focused all of my attention on my husband and my children. I didn't need anyone else. I thought my life was complete.

As my children grew they began to develop friendships at school and sports teams they played on. My husband had his friends to socialize with as well. I had no friends and limited my contact with my immediate family. I was afraid to reach out. I was lonely but I was safe. I just sort of tagged along and remained in the background as if I were invisible. I hoped that if I remained silent, then no one would notice me.

Time moves on and kids grow so fast (So be sure to cherish the time that you have with your kids). My oldest child wanted to stretch her wings and leave the nest. I resisted as much as I could. I wanted my first born to live with us as long as possible. I didn't want her to get hurt by growing up and leaving home. But that day came, and she left. I was so sad and so afraid.

After having lived away from home for a while my daughter began having troubles with her boyfriend. They were fighting and treating each other badly. She called Ganohkwásra[7] and began her counselling to start on her healing path. I thought about what she was doing and how brave she was. Then I began to think about myself. How did I feel about myself? I didn't have any answers. I had no feelings about that question. I thought about the counselling program and wondered if it could help me. I didn't feel good about myself. I didn't like myself. I had no boundaries. I put myself last. I had no voice. I began to feel I was missing something from my life. I was tired of feeling alone, unhappy and detached from my emotions so I began searching for what was missing. I didn't know what it was but I wanted it more and more. Finally I decided to call Ganohkwásra[7]. I was so afraid I almost could not make the call. It was hard but I told them I needed counselling and I wanted to get started.

When I came in for my first visit I was so afraid. I didn't want anyone to see me. I hurried and ran to the door trying to get in before someone could see me. I remember that day so well. I met with the intake worker, filled out the forms and talked for a bit. I didn't go into sexual assault counselling at first. I knew I needed that too but first I needed help to feel better about my relationship with my husband. At the time I was suffering from emotional, spiritual and mental abuse. I had no voice and knew nothing about boundaries or that I mattered.

It was difficult at first, learning to trust myself and develop trust for my counsellor. It went slowly with one word answers leading to short, little sentences. Each time I came in for my session with my individual counsellor, it was as if I had to start from the beginning by talking very little when I had to answer questions. Still, my counsellor was so patient, supportive and understanding. This was what I needed to begin feeling better about myself. Gradually I began to trust myself and open up. I was surprised when I couldn't wait to go to my session. The weeks were going by and I became less afraid of my individual sessions. My counsellor gave me an affirmation book which I read every day. As I read the daily passage, I really felt it inside of me. This helped me to replace the negative thoughts I had about myself and life in general with more positive ones. I was never pushed to try new things until I was ready.

  Concentrating on "me" was the most difficult thing to do. In my sessions, I had to look at my behaviours and how I reacted to things. The only feelings I had ever had and used were anger, fear, sarcasm and shame. I thought negatively of those feelings and didn't want to experience them so I stuffed my feelings, making me a non-feeling, un-reactive person. I had really lost myself by keeping my thoughts and feelings inside, not allowing my true self to be visible to other people. That was the protection I needed and my way of coping with all the sexual assault I had gone through. As a result, I had a lack of social skills; I grew to be untrusting and stayed away from people. I have felt so alone because I never really allowed myself to have any meaningful friendships.

  In counselling, I became more and more aware of who I really am. As I grew more acquainted with myself, I felt better and better. I realized the sexual assault I experienced was not my fault. I had a body that I had lost control of because someone had invaded my boundaries. But as I learned about boundaries in my sessions I came to realize I could have boundaries that were for me. I could control who I allowed in and it was okay to do that. I began to recognize when my boundaries were being violated and I could back away to a safe distance.

  I have learned that I spoke very little because I didn't know how to use my voice. I had kept that inside as well. I had all these thoughts in my head and I wouldn't talk with anyone about them because I believed I had no friends or family I could talk to about my problems. So instead, I did a lot of thinking to myself, many times having a conversation with myself and even answering myself. I had done this for so long that it became natural for me. It was easier to do this than to reach out and trust someone else. I did not want to find a friend because I was afraid to be let down and hurt by someone. So, I believe a big turning point for me was when I began to use my voice. I began to talk and express myself. It was incredible. I had been silent all of my life, carefully observing everything, only having conversations with myself. Now I can speak and know people are listening to me. I no longer need to be quiet and speak only when I am spoken to. Today I can use my voice without having to think about it.

    I went through level 1 and level 2 women's community counselling groups twice, as well as a group for survivors of sexual assault at Ganǫhkwásra[7]. I learned a lot of things about abusive relationships, boundaries, new coping skills, legal issues regarding abusive relationships, self-care, self-esteem, sexual abuse, finding a voice, telling my truth and finding my true self. This was so difficult for me. I had never been a part of a group that I enjoyed. I always saw things I wanted for myself but my fear kept me paralyzed and unable to move except to watch and wish. These groups helped me to feel less like I was so alone. I saw other people who had gone through sexual assault and abusive relationships. I could identify with them. That made us a group. We were survivors. I learned how to trust myself and allowed myself to take risks by reaching out. With each group I took part in, I felt better and better about myself and what I had accomplished.

    In the last two groups I was in, I developed a relationship with the other members. I bonded with them and was glad to see them each week. I never had any sisters, but in this group I had four sisters whom I came to know and trust. One of my counsellors told me that whatever a person needs, be it a brother or sister, they can find people who can fill that need. I am so happy to know my new sisters are there and we can depend on one another.

    There were so many times I could have quit but I didn't. I kept up with my individual counselling sessions and going to groups because I was slowly noticing the changes that were occurring in me. It took a while but I knew I needed to take my time because it had taken me a lifetime to get where I was. At first, the changes were happening without me even realizing it, but I felt better and better about myself. Then, I started to become very aware of each thing I discovered about myself and how each step I took changed the way I felt about myself. I had learned so much and it was beginning to have results. I would feel a new feeling and be afraid but instead of shoving the feeling down, I would feel it, think about it, be with it and then it would be gone. For me, this was amazing.

I am so grateful for the individual and group experiences I have had at Ganohkwásra[7]. The counsellors have been so patient and kind, guiding me along my healing path. They listened to me talk, first with one-word answers, then groups of words and now with sentences. That may sound silly but I needed someone to listen to me. Bear in mind, I was not the easiest person to work with. I would have given up on me a long time ago, but they didn't. They were persistent and would not let me stop, shove my feelings down and be unfeeling. I am so glad that I met these people. With their help, I have discovered the something I had been searching for was me. I am getting to know myself again and I can recognize that I am a person who matters. As a result of reaching out to help myself, I have found my voice and my feelings. I have found my way back to my true self, having some unforgettable experiences and making a few friends along the way.

Trapped

Taken away as a child
Not knowing what was going on,
I have questions to ask,
To find out why,
When can I go home?
I miss my mom,
Will I survive?
Why isn't the sun rising?
Is there going to be another tomorrow?

There's a man who is big and strong,
I get frightened when he comes near,
He touches me and doesn't listen.
Am I mute?
I'm told it's OK to touch, but not to cry,
"Crying is for babies,"
But when he leaves, it just bursts out.
I cry myself to sleep,
But when I wake the pain remains.

The marks on my back that reflect off the mirror, make my eyes water,
I try to look away, but the wounds are deep,
Every move makes them bleed,
The pain makes me scream,
Yet the voice is not heard.
Am I alone?

The face in the mirror is a blur,
Is that me?
Where's my hair, and what's with these clothes?
Who am I?
What's my name?

I was told to be strong for my people,
But the memories make me weak.

The faces I see around me are old, but I seem new.
I scream inside, but not a sound is heard.

I want to be free,
But am forced to stay.
One day I will be free,
But until that day,
I remain here, trapped.

Anonymous

Release your emotions in healthy ways.

If you feel any intense feelings building up, don't hold that energy within your body. Let it out. These feelings take a lot of energy to hold inside the body. If you feel like you just want to scream, do it. Scream into a pillow when you are alone in a room. The pillow will absorb the sound so you won't scare anyone. This is a healthy way to release some of your intense, overwhelming feelings so it doesn't hurt you or anyone else.

Holding in anger will take a toll on the body. It will manifest as pain, numbness and/or physical illness. Karate punches are a technique used in Psychodramatic Bodywork®. When we release our anger we are no longer using our energy to suppress it therefore our energy is free to be used in more healthy ways. Also, when we release our anger, we are less likely to direct it at someone or something in unhealthy or destructive ways. Karate punches are one way of dealing with anger in a healing way. However, this self-care technique is not considered a full anger release. Full anger releases should only be done with a qualified, trained professional.

1. Keep your feet parallel.
2. Bend your knees.
3. Focus your eyes ahead of you.
4. With your elbows bent, inner arms touching your sides, make fists (fingers clutched facing the ceiling)
5. As you punch directly forward into the air in front of you, turn your fist so the back of your hand (fist) now faces the ceiling.
6. Make a loud "HA!" sound with each punch. Return your arm back to your side (step # 4) and punch outward with the other fist.
7. Continue punching until you feel complete.
8. Expect to feel heat and energy before and after the exercise.

This is a healthy and fun technique to teach your children as well.

"I am learning a new way of life"

"I am learning a new way of life."

A few weeks ago I was asked to share my story of sexual abuse and addiction. In the beginning, I felt honoured to be thought of and scared of my limited perception of self and others. My counsellor said, "This means you can tell your story, the one that was never told." I felt such a surge of energy within me. I felt such empowerment. Now that the time is here, there seems to be so many things unsaid and unseen, damaged and broken. I am glad this is a healing journey, one that encompasses feelings of happiness, joy, and sadness due to trauma, loss, grief, and masks of fear that have been my task to uncover.

I remember walking down the city street after having been raped and the only feelings I could identify were incredible guilt, incredible shame and incredible remorse for just about everything that I had encountered in life. I wondered how life could be so bad. How could I feel so bad about life at such an early age? I couldn't understand that for the life of me. I would go to see counsellors and they would ask me what brought me here and I would say, "I don't know. I just feel bad, all pent up, unable to do anything right." I was in trouble, out of school, I'd gotten abused in my childhood and raped in my early teens and yet, I didn't know why I felt so bad.

I grew up off the reserve, in a house with a white picket fence, something out of a fairytale. Actually, it isn't far from the reserve but I didn't learn how distant it could be until later on when I pursued the Native side of my existence.

When I was seven years old, I can remember feeling so scared and praying to God to make it stop but He never answered and as time went on, in that house at least, whatever I was looking for "to make it stop" never came. The "it" was the chaos, the beatings, the yelling, the feelings of worthlessness, nothingness, fear, terrifying fear and the vulnerability in never knowing where the verbal or physical abuse would come from next.

At home I cleaned the house, cooked supper for six people, got my brothers off to school with something in their tummies and then went to school myself. At night, I did my laundry. Mom quit cleaning my linen because I used to pee my bed almost every night. I could smell the stench of urine in my sheets. Later on, I would do any of the laundry that was downstairs in the basement.

It was difficult to know what we did right and what we did wrong. The backroom became "our whipping station." Mom did some pretty mean things to us. I remember that my brother was the scapegoat of the family and I felt it was better that he was back there than me. The fear of what was going to happen to me was just so great that it was like an automatic response to do anything to get out of the punishment.

Abuse came in many forms back then, from strapping to standing in the corner for long periods of time. Sometimes we were made to eat hot peppers or kneel on the end of a broom stick or hot air register. The crime never fit the punishment and all I can remember is never feeling cared for, loved, or wanted. I was always scared of my mom. I never knew what I was going to miss or do or not do to experience her hostility. I just could never make the right move or do the right things. All I remember is being so afraid of her. I guess that's why I always kept busy. I thought that if I worked a little harder, tried a little harder, things might be okay but they never were.

I never knew what was going to happen, never. Sometimes everything would be so good. Dad would play ball with us and we'd walk to gramma's house or along the river. Dad liked doing things with us but sometimes he would walk around the house and talk about how he wished he was dead. I didn't know what to do and couldn't figure out why he would say those things. I never knew if it was because of me or us kids or what. I just never knew what was causing him so much pain that he wanted to be dead, but I could see it on his face.

Both my parents drank and when friends would come over, everything somehow seemed to be different. There was no tension on mom and dad's faces, no cursing words from my mother or anything. Dad liked country and western music and so did his friends. Most of his friends played country and western music on their guitars and fiddles. I got to choose which record would be played on the record player and Dad always asked me or one of my brothers to "get Dad a beer out of the fridge." I remember we would always jump to get one for him, so willing to please. When Mom and Dad's friends were over, Mom and Dad would give us twenty-five or fifty cents to go to the corner store for a treat. We would walk two and a half concessions to do that, often being gone for a couple of hours at a time. But what I remember mostly is that Mom and Dad seemed to be happy. They would be drinking and there didn't seem to be that tension that would otherwise be on their faces.

Coming from an alcoholic home, I pretty much had grown up with drinking. My folks have drank for as long as I can remember. My maternal grandparents drank and so did my aunts and uncles on my mom's side. My father was the main drinker on his side. There were times in my life when dad would fall down and bruise himself really bad then ask me why I hit him. I can also remember driving the old '59 Fargo home because dad was too drunk to drive himself. I would be scared out of my wits of hitting something or being pulled over by the cops. When we were in our teens my brothers and I drank with our dad. He preferred we drink with him, in his house, so that nothing bad would happen. On the other hand, Mom wouldn't allow us to drink at home. To allow it meant condoning it and she wanted no part of that.

I can remember my brothers and I sneaking beer and treats out of the old refrigerator at home before the age of twelve, wanting to be like the big people. We were always getting into deep trouble for that. When we started to steal cigarettes mom would make us sit down with her and smoke cigarettes, drink beer and eat cookies to try curtail our new interests. I can remember getting so sick. Mom's tactics didn't work though. No matter how much she tried it didn't stop me, or my brothers, from smoking or drinking.

When my parents split up my brothers and I moved to the city with my mom. At first mom worked then she went to hair dressing school and started dating. Dad seldom came around and it felt as though everything was gone. Everything I knew and loved died and so did I. I hungered for love, for attention and comfort, and for all of those things that come with it like stability and security. I would sit or walk in a daze waiting, wanting, yearning for someone to notice that I was so sad and alone but no one ever did. I was thirteen.

In the city, things were so different. There were a lot more boys around. When we lived in the country, we would go swimming and there would be boys around. I don't know where I learned this from, but I would slide my bathing suit strap off my shoulder to grab the boys' attention or I would stuff my bra. Looking back I think it was just me developing sexually and needing attention so badly. I had been sexually abused as a small child so I learned really young that I could get attention using my sexuality. I'll never know what those young boys from the country thought but it seemed they never took notice. In the city when I would wiggle my bum or flirt with the boys it was very much noticed. Without much guidance or supervision, I didn't know I could acquaint myself with the "wrong men." I was just beginning to blossom and these were boys in their later teens.

One night while Mom and the boys were out, I called an acquaintance where there was a party going on. Wanting to be a part of this crowd I edged them on sexually. A couple of the boys came to the house. I hadn't really wanted to be sexual with them, I just wanted to fit in. I said I'd lock the door, but one of the boys said that if I didn't unlock it they would break it down. All I could think of was if they broke the door down my mom would be furious. So I opened the door and they came in. We went in my bedroom and at knifepoint I took off my pants. One of the boys climbed on top of me while the other held the knife. When the first was finished he motioned to the other to have his turn. I remember not being able to fathom someone else on top of me and I snapped. I started swirling around in my room, screaming and yelling. They took off and without me noticing, they took my guitar that my mom had bought me for Christmas. It was a beautiful, electric acoustic guitar. I was fourteen. I remember wondering if it was rape. Was I raped? They hurt me so bad but I had invited them over.

Later on that summer, I ran into other guys that hung around with the ones who had raped me. I was still a flirtatious young woman and when I was invited into the bedroom I accepted. I didn't expect anything to happen like it did. No sooner were we on the bed when he started to get rough with me.

The rougher he got the more I yelled and he told me that if I didn't stop screaming he would kill me. The penetration hurt so bad but I stopped screaming and took it. After he finished I got dressed and laid down beside the chesterfield and fell asleep. I didn't have the energy or the strength to go home. Why would I go home anyway, when there was nothing there? I wanted to be dead. I wanted to be invisible. I just wanted to be gone.

In grade eight, I met the girl who would be my best friend my first few years in town. She was my "introducer". She's the one I started to drink and drug with. For whatever reasons she always knew when it was time to go but not me. It took so much to escape the pain inside of me, yet I couldn't stop because I wouldn't give up trying.

Years ago everyone would hang around at Harvey's. One evening when I was there this guy asked me if I would like to go for a ride. I said, "Okay." For the life of me I don't remember what we talked about but I remember what he did. He took me to the country on some dark, deserted road. He parked the car and wherever we were there were other guys there too. All I remember is this one guy saying, "Well, look what we have here." I could hear more than one male voice outside of the car and instantly felt an overwhelming fear that engulfed me from that second on. I don't recall everyone that was there but I do remember some of them. Some of them who got in that back seat raped me. Others would come in and say, "Shhh, don't say anything." They would be there just long enough for a pretended "quicky" and leave. I don't remember who dropped me off and I don't care. I got home at two o'clock in the morning. My mom was awake and gave me heck for coming in so late. I walked out the door and ended up at a friend's house. I asked him if I could stay the night and I sobbed my heart out. He never asked why and I was too tired to say. From that moment on I hated my mother. She never asked why I had come in late. She just started yelling. I couldn't take that, not with what had happened that night.

After that I started blacking out around the rapes and didn't care what boy had me or where. Before my sobriety, which came many years later, I couldn't tell you how many boys, guys, or men that I had slept with for some kind of love or attention, something that let me know I was real. It all seemed to be such a haze and one I succumbed to. It just didn't seem to matter anymore. As long as there was alcohol to numb the pain, who cared?

At the end of my sixteen years, I was living on the street pretty much. That's where I felt most comfortable and most accepted. Once, I ran into a fellow I knew from the neighbourhood. We found an old abandoned car and before I knew it, it was over and I was at the doctor's office with a positive pregnancy test. My son was born in January 1977 and three months later, he was in care of the Children's Aid Society. Everything I knew and/or cared about would not be enough for this darling, precious baby boy. One day, a CAS worker who had been involved with my family (brothers mostly), said, "A child needs love, stability and security." I realized right then what I was called to do so I signed adoption papers. For all the things in my life that had happened I couldn't come close to what I knew he needed or would need from me. I had so many intense and mixed emotions about the whole thing. I'm surprised I came through it. The adoption became final a year after his birth. After the court proceedings, I remember walking out of City Hall and a friend asking me if I would be alright. I said, "Yeah," but even now I'm not sure what that meant. I had just given away the only person in life that really mattered to me.

Later on, I met a young man who was involved in pharmacy break and enters. I started taking pills and got involved with using IV drugs while I continued to drink. I used methamphetamines mostly. I remember the first time I got high off them and not thinking much about it but later on it would become my drug of choice. I was seventeen years old.

Over the next five years, times were pretty intense. The police were often on our trail (or tail). Everyone was getting all screwed up on the speed and somewhere in between I ended up pregnant again. I aborted in my drinking while going to see the baby's father and him not being home. There was child number two, gone. Just like that. Don't ask me how old I was, I couldn't tell you, but I think somewhere between the ages of twenty-one or twenty-two.

In the next five years, I got pregnant again but I didn't know who the father was. I was living with a life long friend of mine who had kept her three children. I, on the other hand, aborted one more time. I just couldn't go through the stereotyping and the opinions and judgements from other people. It was then that I dammed God to hell and turned myself away from Him. I was twenty-six or twenty-seven years old.

For the next two years I drank and did every drug I could get my hands on. I didn't get into too many "downs" because once I'd seen a man like that in a hotel. He had been on some kind of downers and was frothing at the mouth. He had urinated on himself. I always remember that image of him as being what I never wanted to look like. I loathed him.

I reached a point where I'd lost everything I'd ever owned materialistically and with the hopes of my baby boy being gone I lost everything internally as well. Plus, the only man I ever loved was in prison again. In a drunken blind rage I went to the mall to steal pots, pans, and dishes. Those were the things I needed to set up a home. I got caught and left the scene scared to death. I took back my friend's car that I had borrowed. It was all so scary. I knew I was in trouble with the law this time. After about six months I walked the streets wondering when they would catch up with me. Having that fear in me, I started to think about my life, about what happened at the mall, the rapes and my family life, I started to think if I didn't soon stop and do something I was going to go to jail for a very long time for the crime I had just committed. In my heart, I knew I could never survive prison because of all the things that happened to me. I knew what it felt like to have pain imposed on me from the anger and hurt of another. I needed to get help and I needed to go to Alcoholics Anonymous.

In 1988, I started going back to school. Having never obtained any courses in high school when I was young I always wanted to go back to get an education and so I did. One day while I was leaving class a police officer was waiting for me outside the high school. He was in an unmarked car. In a futile attempt I turned to go off in the other direction but he called me over. He got out of his seat and opened the back door of the cruiser for me to sit in. As I sat down the door was closed and I was under arrest as he was reading me my rights. I tried to deny it for a while but underneath I was too scared of what was going to happen to me. I was relieved that it had finally come to an end. I got charged with criminal negligence and before I went to court a pre-sentence report was drawn up. I don't know what, where or how, but one evening in my most desperate and loneliest of times, AA popped into my head and I went to an AA meeting in 1988.

My first dry date was November 11, 1988. I stopped drinking for the first time, in what I can recall my whole life, for about six months and just from going to AA meetings. I didn't read the big book, I didn't get a sponsor. I didn't deal with my fear or the trauma of being raped. I didn't change my thinking or the people I hung around with but I was relieved that everything wasn't so crazy.

After everything settled down, I started having thoughts of drinking and I started using again. I tried drinking stuff like wine coolers instead of beer or whiskey and I smoked the odd joint but otherwise left everything else alone. Still, about eighteen months into my using again I woke up and I didn't know if it was morning or night. This voice inside me said, "You know a place that's safe." I said, "Yeah. AA." At that moment I knew that I had to go back. It was a Sunday morning and I had been on a four day spree, waking up and drinking which was something I didn't normally do.

After another relationship ended and a four day bender, I attended my first meeting for the second time on May 8th, 1990. This time I went to AA faithfully, sometimes 10 to 14 meetings a week. I was just so terrified to be anywhere but an AA meeting or with people from within the program. They knew, like I did, the harmful, destructive ways of alcoholism and as long as I was there I never did IV drugs and to this day never have. AA would say, you got to be "H.O.W." – honest, open-minded, and willing. Only God knows how willing I became. There wasn't anything that I wouldn't do for AA. If someone asked me to speak, I did it. If someone asked me to clean, I did it. If they said go back to doing 90 meetings in 90 days, I did it. After awhile, I did it without being told. And after awhile, I would feel good about myself for not drinking and using drugs but I still didn't feel good about myself overall. It just seemed that nothing could take away the way I innately felt about my "own" person. My thoughts wouldn't stop coming. In the end I knew that no matter how much I learned in school (college, university), it was real life that counted, and I had a whole lot of hurt, destruction and inability to deal with my abuse. I knew I had to pursue counselling or I would turn back to the alcohol and drugs.

I soaked myself in AA, attending meetings, chairing meetings, reading the big book, getting a sponsor and helping out where I could. The first time I spoke my story lasted about twelve minutes. I thought it was great to even begin to bring some light into the darkness no matter how small. Thank God the Creator looks at the small attempts we do try. I would not have survived the dread of what did manage to come out.

One of the other things that I did was to apply to college in December of 1989. I was accepted into a two year social work program at Mohawk College. In that program, I came to learn an holistic approach to physical, emotional, mental, and spiritual well-being. Because I was still drinking when I was considering the program, I also realized if I didn't stop drinking there was no way that I would get through the program successfully. Having tried to stop my alcohol use and abuse in the past, I learned I wasn't able to do it without help so I went back to AA and decided to stay. Thank God I did.

In September 1990, I started college and despite everything I'd ever known about education, I loved what I was doing. So many times in my life I asked questions about why is this or why is that and I was always told it wasn't important. In this program I learned that those little questions were important and that I should never let anyone ever tell me different again. I loved it. I loved learning. It was opening me up to another horizon, a newer level of living, of life. Lord knows how much I needed that. I was happy about knowing that. Even with crisis in my life, I passed first year on the Dean's List. Later on, the next year, I passed on the Dean's List again, making me an honour's graduate. I was tickled pink and so proud of myself.

I remember sitting in class one day and we had someone

come in and talk about sexual abuse. I learned something that hit hard on the mark. This woman was talking about teachings and what we learn from one another and how we keep learning by sharing. Then, she talked about the woman's uterus being like her home and a woman's vagina being the door to her home. She went on to explain that a woman could let in whomever she wanted, when she wanted, as she wanted, and I realized that day that I could have some control over my home. Somehow, hearing a woman share that empowered me and I have never acted in the same manner since.

When the second term of my studies was coming to a close I started to feel really saddened about leaving the place that had taught me so much and given me so much of my self. Between college, AA and of course, counselling, I had turned around so much of my life to a better life and I couldn't help but feel amiss of what I was about to leave behind. On the other hand, I wanted more than a college diploma because I wanted to go all the way, to university.

I kept attending AA meetings to keep me sober and a little to my surprise, even stopped smoking for a while. I worked that summer and completed an application for Western University. As an adolescent I had always dreamed about going to Western U and after graduating with honours from Mohawk, I pretty much had the pick of the crop. So I packed up and moved to London and started my first year at my dream school, UWO.

Having left high school with no senior English classes my papers suffered greatly since I didn't know how to present my arguments. I continued full speed ahead until the end of the year but inside I knew that being away from friends, family, my home, and all the people who loved and cared for me, I was at a loss. That summer, I came home and lived with a couple in AA. I felt too different so I left and stayed with my grandfather while I worked. He didn't understand me, or my spending habits, and ended up giving me three days to leave. After that summer I felt on shaky ground, almost dreading the experience of having to go back to London to fulfill the year ahead of me, but I did. I didn't feel I had the energy needed, physically or emotionally, but I went back.

About mid-term I started having trouble with stress and depression crept in. I started to fear that if I didn't go to the university doctor to get some anti-depressants, I would lose the school year and about $8,000. I prayed to God that didn't happen. I tried to continue through until the end of my term. I remember going to my father's that year at Christmas and returning to London at the end of it, but between Christmas and the New Year, I had begun drinking and using IV drugs again, cocaine and speed. I'd lost my 3.5 years of sobriety and clean time. It just felt like everything was piling up and I had no time or inkling of how to cope with my life. So, in the winter of 1994 I left my studies with no penalty at the University.

In my late twenties I had went to a sexual assault and family violence centre in town. I stayed there for quite a while as they helped a lot with my childhood abuse and, to some degree, with being raped. After attending for three years I felt it was time to be on my way, but I ended up going back because things were piling up on me again with my anger and noted, violent past. This next time at counselling did not go well. The counsellor just wasn't able to show me how to get through what I needed to get through. Now I know that people who have been sexually abused need be able to yell and scream to release the pent up fear, anger and rage that is inside of them. At that time, none of the counsellors there seemed supportive of allowing me to do that.

One day I was talking with a friend of mine who was seeking counselling at Ganohkwásra[7]. He said they knew him so well, even more than he knew himself. I thought of my insides and how much I needed that too if I wanted to get past the isolation and desolate feelings I had. I knew that somewhere there had to be an organization, a place, a counsellor, that could deal with me. When my friend told me how much they had helped him at Ganohkwasra, I thought, "I'm going to go there someday."

Well that day came sooner than I expected. Actually it took longer than I thought it would, but finally I was in the doors of Ganohkwásra[7] and began meeting with the counsellor that today, is very much helping me to learn how to take care of myself and allow myself to heal while taking the time that I need to get better. And, I am getting better.

I remember not being able to talk when I got to Ganohkwásra'. I was so occupied with keeping my feelings under check and listening to my thoughts passing my mind that to talk took a lot of concentration. At least Ganohkwásra' understood that. They understood the dam that was holding everything in and they understood about suffering from debilitating shame and guilt. They understood what being violently raped had done to my mind, body and spirit.

My counsellor helped me to recognize that I would never totally be successful in my sobriety until I dealt with the trauma of being sexually assaulted. So today, with the help of Ganohkwásra' I understand the need for emotional releases.* I understand the urgency behind them and the power within them, the vision in front of them and the voice that follows them. I look forward to the day when I don't have a need for them. Until that day comes, however, I will welcome and be thankful for every one.

For one of my sessions I met in the gym with the sexual assault counsellors to do some EMDR work.* This was a process of letting my soul travel where it wanted to. I ended up touching so many vulnerable parts inside of me: the rapes, the emotional chaos, the picture of that violence, that ever so large emptiness of children come and gone. So many things separated me from this world and the people in it. I never thought that in the near future I would experience the wonderful gift of not feeling afraid and knowing that I will be alright.

Since I've been at Ganohkwásra' I have been learning what it means to be sexually assaulted against your will. Today, no one will ever take my voice away from me again. I learned how to unblock the walls that kept me separate from the real part of me. I have learned why I do the things I do, why I feel the way I feel. I can understand the emptiness inside me and the extreme parts of myself. These things have been very hard things to work through because I have had so much fear.

I am also learning how to take care of me, something no

---

* For a brief description of emotional release work refer to "Psychodramatic Bodywork" on p.203
* Please refer to p. 204 for a description of EMDR—Eye Movement Desensitization and Reprocessing

one ever cared enough to show me. It's not about abusing myself with alcohol or drugs or abusing others through angry outbursts. It's about caring for me in this moment and how I feel while doing that and being willing to overcome these things enough that I can work through them. I am learning that I am an okay person, an exceptional person even. I am a person who has had a tenacious backbone to continue to work through the issues that blind me from thinking and feeling positive about myself.

I remember when I first started working on my life in AA. If I remembered to just take baby steps, I could manage me in my life, just for today. I didn't have to impress anybody except me. At night time I would ask myself, "Did you do the best you could do, just for today?" Then I would look at my day in a spiritual sense and be content in knowing that, "yes I did." If there were nights where I couldn't say "yes," I would only say to myself, "Tomorrow is another day and you can try again." I wouldn't beat myself up.

I remember not having a sense of connectedness with my higher power yet when I would see the trees move and the leaves dance when the wind would blow and I would say to myself that this is how the higher power works in our lives. I couldn't see Him, but I could feel his presence on my face, in nature, and in the good deeds and acts that people did and my concept began to grow. I can remember feeling like a small child. No one was there to protect me and how, as more adversity came to me as a young adolescent, I really held a child's view of the Creator. My inner child felt that God was supposed to be there for me for everything. Then, when God wasn't there for me, I turned my back on Him. Those were the worst times in my life. I didn't know what I was doing when I did that. All I knew was how worse my life was from having done that.

Learning to identify with the child that lost her innocence from a life full of sexual interference has been a very difficult thing to unfold. I didn't think much of it when a boy put his hand down my pants in the garage to "feel my monkey," but the event always popped into my head intermittently through the years. Maybe I haven't given that incident the attention it deserves because, after being violently raped, I thought it wasn't really anything. I'd also forgotten about the times that my uncle would sit me on his knee and fondle my boobs and rub me. He actually encouraged me to perform oral sex on him and I can still remember wanting to please him while servicing him and him telling me, "Not so hard." He's dead now. Sometimes I wish he wasn't. I'd like to talk to him. Long before the abuse, he was nice to me. Even when my mom was mean to me, he made me feel better about myself. I recognize now that those times are worth talking about too because they are just simpler forms of being taken advantage of sexually. Those times didn't hurt me the way others would physically, sexually, emotionally, mentally and spiritually, but those people were responsible for the actions they passed on to me. Still, I can be grateful now because at least I know how I think and feel towards them.

All of these things I have learned have helped me so much. And I am continuing to learn with the help of Ganǫhkwásra'. I think Ganǫhkwásra' is a very special place. The people there are so humble in their individual presence to hear and take care of information divulged to them and to ask the Creator, "What is troubling this person today and how can I help them?" That is such a rare and special thing to do.

My counsellor holds my emotions, my thoughts, my very security and safeness, in the palm of her hands. She handles me with care, respect and an insurmountable amount of gentleness and love. Before I came to Ganǫhkwásra' no one ever taught me that I could have boundaries and limits for myself, amongst others, or between myself and other people. No one ever cared enough to show me these things mattered, but Ganǫhkwásra' did. They continue to show me how to take care of myself. If I am feeling this way or that, I know what to do when I leave there and what actions I need to follow through with in order to take care of myself with respect. Slowly, I am learning about self–respect and what that means.

Ganǫhkwásra' is helping me to become the person that I am, not who I pretend to be or want to be, but who I really am. They help me deal with my anger, my sadness, my rage and my confusion so that my life can be a healthy one. I still have a long way to go but it's more than just a glimpse today. I really believe that I am becoming someone that has a true sense of herself. I'm not someone that other people conjured up to protect their being. I am becoming "me." This has been the most beautiful gift that I have received from going to Ganǫhkwásra'. I have my very own sense of self. I feel her, sense her. She is with me wherever I go and she is a marvellous delight. I am learning to connect to all parts of that self.

After years of counselling, I still feel awful most times, sad and scared mostly, but lonely too. But, today, I realize that I am not able to be in a healthy, caring relationship at this time. I know that I am learning, or trying to learn, a new way of life, a life with love, caring and sharing. Yet sometimes that isn't at all how I feel. My fear can still turn to anger because in my childhood years I was not able to express my anger or my fear. If I was fearful there was no one there to hug me, comfort me or tell me how special I was and that we would get through this together. I was sent to my room or outside to play and that was how it was. I learned rejection and abandonment by how I felt, emotionally and mentally, and I would do anything to prevent an injection of that type of pain. I was always more than terrified.

I don't blame my parents anymore for how I was raised. I am learning to detach from them. They did the best they could and I am learning to accept that. It doesn't mean that I don't love them because I do. However, our paths will never cross on our healing journeys because I am the only one in my family on a healing and/or recovery journey. Still, my family is doing a lot better. My father hasn't had a drink in ten years and my mother has quit drinking as well. One of the highlights of my healing has been for my mother and I to buy a house together. Together. We've come a long way from the way things were when I was a child but we still have a long way to go. We are learning how to do more than just survive, we are learning how to live. Despite troubles with depression, my family is doing the best we can. To me, that's a miracle and I thank the Creator for what He has given us.

In 2000, I was diagnosed with having Hepatitis C, a result of my IV drug use. Since then, knowing about the chronic illness, I find it hard to ignore the consequences it has had on me.

I was also diagnosed with diabetes at that time. This year, 2004, I was diagnosed with having Post Traumatic Stress Disorder, the long-term effect of having been raped at knife point and with having my life threatened. The rapes have not been an easy thing for me to get through and I do a lot of grief work over the things I have lost throughout my life as a result.

In the past two years, my work to heal from sexual trauma has become more intensified due to having the appropriate team of people helping me to work through the personal relationships and the emotional, sexual, self-esteem and self-image problems that manifested over a period of years. One day, I hope that all of my actions come from a caring, healthy person who is me. I hope I can trust myself and the decisions I make about my health and welfare. I believe I will come to a place where I will know what is good for me because I really, truly do care about how and where I spend my total existence.

I Forgive You

I forgive you.
My forgiveness is not about you.
It is about me.
I am only responsible for me.
I will not hate you. I will not resent you.
If I do, my heart will never heal.

I can not look to you for forgiveness.
I can only apologize for my wrong doings.
You must take care of you.
Your actions are not my responsibility.
That is between you and Sonkwaya'tihson.
I will let him guide your healing.

To forgive means letting go of the pain.
I've grieved my losses and mended my broken heart.
Today, I see the light of Creator's love.
I know my spirit is a part of him.
And, you are also a part of the universal love that connects each of us.
I can love you again because I have learned to love me again.

What else matters?

S. L. Hill, 2004

Contain your feelings in a safe place until you are able to address them

Imagine your feelings are being put away in a container where you feel they are safe. Promise yourself that you will not forget about putting these feelings away and that you will take them out to deal with them at a more appropriate time. You may even want to identify the appropriate time to ensure you will not forget about addressing these feelings.

You can also create for your self an actual "containment box." Write down your feelings in a short and simple form and put the paper in the box. When you are ready to address those feelings or perhaps when you see your counsellor or therapist, you can take the paper(s) out and address them as necessary.

"I can stop leaving my body now"

I remember a time when I was with friends. We were reminiscing about the teachers we had in grade school. When it came around to my turn, all I could remember was my kindergarten teacher and my grade one teacher. I realized I remembered very little about my grade school years. This was my first clue that something was wrong.

One evening I was in a very frightening situation where I was being followed and harassed by a man. When I finally managed to get away from him, I could not remember what he looked like. I could not remember where I had been after he started to bother me. The only thing I remembered was going into a drug store and asking for help and they refused. Something was very wrong. I realized whenever I was under any kind of stress I would "take off" or, in other words, spiritually leave my body. This was not good; I was leaving myself open to danger.

It took me a few years to get up the courage to seek help. I tried many different organizations and people, but no one seemed to be able to help me. All they would do is put a band-aid on the problem and it would just creep back up later.

Six years ago, I walked into the office of a counsellor at Ganǫhkwásra' to seek help as a victim of sexual abuse. I was a shy girl with very little self-worth or self-esteem. I was afraid to make decisions and I was always giving in to everyone else, even when it hurt me. I had problems recognizing and expressing my feelings, especially grief and pain, both of my body and my soul. I didn't know who I was or what I wanted.

I remember very little before the instances of sexual abuse started to happen. I think this is because of my dissociation and that I was so young when the abuse started. My mother went back to working full-time when I was about two and a half years old. My parents decided to bring in a live-in nanny. I did not like the nanny. She ignored me completely and only played with my younger sister. When my younger sister went down for a nap, I thought maybe she would finally play with me. I was wrong. She told me to be quiet, not to make any noise and just sit there. I was not even allowed to play quietly by myself. This was the first time I felt real loneliness. I have never felt that lonely since. I was three and a half years old and I wanted to die. I wanted someone to pay attention to me. After I started school full-time my parents dismissed the nanny, arranging for someone else to look after us before and after school. This was when the sexual abuse first started.

I was repeatedly sexually abused from the age of four to sixteen. I do not remember all of the occurrences as distinct instances. Most of them seem to blur together as one. The experience I remember the most was when I was about five. I was sexually abused before I went to school that day. I was taken into a bedroom and blindfolded. My perpetrator would perform oral sex on me while he masturbated. As a result of this instance of abuse I did not have enough time to get ready for school. I went to school without my hair being brushed. It was picture day for my grade one class and now, whenever I look at that picture I feel very sad. I feel sad for the lost, scared, alone child that I was in that picture. I can see it in my eyes.

Another traumatic memory I have is from a child's perspective. My abuser told me he was going to do something different. As a child, my memory was that he tried to stuff a balloon in my vagina with his finger and blow it up. I was screaming with pain. He kept trying until he could not stand the screaming anymore. As an adult, I now realize this was him putting his condom covered penis inside of me. I am forty now and I just realized a few years ago what this memory actually represented.

I loved and idolized my abuser. He was related to me and was much older than me. Everyone liked him. I loved it when he paid any attention to me. When the abuse first started, I was four years old. We were playing together when he asked me if he could "lick my bum." I laughed and then I realized he was serious. I said okay. I didn't know what he meant but all I know was I didn't want to do anything to get out of his favour. Once it started, it felt wrong and I did not like it. I dreaded it. He always told me not to tell anyone. I knew if I told he would get in trouble. I loved him and I did not want to see him get hurt so I didn't tell. The abuse went on for years. It did not stop until I was sixteen years old.

I worry that my perpetrator will abuse someone else. I

worry about his kids. I still have not told the police or his wife. I do not want to ruin his life for something he did while he was young. In that way, I am still protecting him. After I was on my healing journey I confronted him. I asked him why he did it. He could not answer me. I told him I still loved him and I forgave him. I told him it really affected my life. I told him I wanted him to get help and he better not do it again or I would tell the authorities. I told him if anyone ever said that it was happening to them, I would believe them and I would be on their side. They would not have to testify because I would. I would make sure he went behind bars. I still worry today if I made the right decision by not telling the authorities. I hope my fear is never realized.

As a child, I was very shy. I did not want to have to talk to people. I always felt I was on the outside, even in kindergarten. When all of the kids were playing together I would play by myself. I remember one of the things I wanted the most was to live up north in the middle of nowhere. I wanted to be as far away from people as I could possibly be. My abuse continued throughout the years not only by my main abuser, but also by a close friend of the family. He would touch me any opportunity he had. I was finally able to tell my mother about this. She told me to go to a neighbour's house whenever he came over and no one else was home with me. This did put an end to the abuse. I am upset that the person is still a family friend, not as close as before but still a friend. Nothing was said to him about the abuse. I was just told how to get away from it.

The sexual abuse affected me in a lot of ways. I did not like to be touched; not even hugged by my parents. I avoided all physical contact and recoiled at any accidental touch. Before I had my own room I could not sleep through the night and when I did sleep it was only a half sleep. The slightest sound, such as the sound of the cat's claws clicking on the floor when it walked into my room would wake me up. I did not sleep through the night without waking up until I received my own bedroom with a lock on the door.

Another way the abuse really affected me was I did not want to grow up. When I started to go through puberty changes I would try to hide. I cut off my pubic hair. I refused to wear bras.

I would just wear large shirts with layers underneath. I would not wash my hair or wear makeup. I wore clothes that were out of date. I did everything possible not to be attractive. I did not try to look better until the girls at school started to make fun of me. That was too much to bear, so I started to try to look at least presentable.

My first relationship with a boy was abusive as well. At first it seemed okay but then it just got more and more abusive. We had a sexual relationship. We would make out in the car. I usually had to go to pee afterwards. I would go in the bushes and he would start the car and shine the lights on me. This was very embarrassing. He would also tell lies to his friends about me. He would tell them that I would play with myself. One time when we got in a car accident, he told everyone I did it. He even tried to convince the police, but they had seen him in the driver's seat, so they did not believe him. He was so convincing that I started to have trouble recognizing the truth from the lies. I had started college and he took me to his professor and told them to change my major. He did all the talking. They changed it, without even asking what I wanted. I was too scared to speak up in the office. I was lucky to get out of that relationship. The only reason I did was because he found someone else.

Before I received help as a victim of sexual abuse, I had very low self-esteem. I thought I was very ugly, boring and not very smart. I just wanted to be loved. I was happy when any male showed attention to me other than just being friends. I had a lot of male friends, but no one I thought who was interested in me. I would endure the abusive treatment because I thought I was not worthy of any other treatment. Having grown up watching my parents' healthy relationship I knew the treatment I was receiving was not normal. It was very hard for me to get up the courage and strength to get out of the abusive relationships. I wanted to be loved and I feared no one else would want me. This spilled over into female friendships. I thought I was boring and no one would want to talk to me. I believed I had nothing to contribute to any conversation. I was only good for helping with what they needed.

In my healing journey I have realized that I am someone

people want to get to know. I have learned to say "no" and stick up for myself. I have also learned that there were a few nice men who wanted to date me when I was young. My self-confidence was so low, that it would not allow me to see it. One fellow in particular came to my house everyday and took me to hockey games and shopping and whatever we wanted to do. He taught me to play the guitar. He was always a perfect gentleman. I thought he was just being a friend and had no interest in me any more than that. It was during this time I met the man I had the abusive relationship with. I never saw the perfect gentlemen again. I did not understand why he stopped visiting me until years later when I was told he was interested in me as more than a friend. I regret not realizing this. He was a very nice man and I would have dated him in an instant. I feel sad; I must have really hurt his feelings.

  The next man I had a relationship with, I married. I did not realize that he was abusive to me as well. My sister tried to warn me, but I could not see it. He was verbally and later physically abusive. He was a drug addict and alcoholic. He was very abusive to me when he was under the influence. He did not trust me and made me stop hanging out with my friends unless he was present. I lost myself in that relationship. I was not a strong person to begin with, but I almost gave up. I was diagnosed with fibermyalgia. I was always sick with pneumonia and asthma. I knew if things did not change I would die. I looked very old. I was mentally worn out. I was even scared to drive a car. I told my husband to get help for his addictions or I would leave him. I said I would stay with him and help him through it. I knew I needed to make myself strong in order to help him so I started to do things for me. I started with cooking classes and later I joined a gym. This went on for two years. I had regained some of my strength yet he had not made any progress with his addictions.

  I went to see a counsellor who was associated with my place of employment. They were not able to help me much. I told them a little about the childhood sexual abuse, but they seemed only interested in helping me with my immediate problems. They did not get to the root of the problem that was bothering me. They just told me to leave my husband and to pull myself together. After I left my husband, I went back to the counsellor. I was still having trouble. They just dismissed it. Finally, a friend told me about a counsellor at **Ganohkwasra**. She thought they could help me there.

At **Ganǫhkwásra**[7], I entered into the sexual assault program. It was there I learned about my "taking off," or as I have learned it is called, dissociation. Dissociation is a tool I developed as a child to protect myself. I used it before the abuse started, whenever I would get nervous or scared. I used it more and it went to deeper levels during my sexual assaults. I would not be present in my body to remember or feel the pain. I did not remember all of what happened at all of the occurrences. After a few times of the abuse happening I would start to take off as soon as it started again. Only part of me was left there to experience the pain, degradation, helplessness, loneliness and anger. The "taking off" started to spread into the rest of my life. Anytime I started to feel any stress I would take off. This could be as little as the stress of walking into a crowded room.

For me dissociation was an escape to a peaceful place. I would know it was happening again when I would feel a prickly feeling on the back of my neck. My vision would start to become distorted. The world would start to sway. Then I would see things clearly again, but I would not be seeing it from the view that my eyes would see. Sometimes, I would be up above and ahead of where I was physically located. If I were walking I would see things far ahead that I could not possibly see from where I was standing. If the situation was traumatic enough I would go to a completely different place and time. I would often go to a place where there were rolling hills covered with trees and an open meadow. I would ride a horse along this huge expanse of barren land – I loved it. I had no sense at all of what was happening around me or to my body during the times I left.

I "took off" so much it eventually took over my life and I was hardly ever in the present. People I had apparently met would come up and talk with me, but I would not remember ever having met them. Sometimes I would remember later. This one time, my brother and I were walking home and there were some kids fighting at school. We stopped to watch. My brother saw that the boy's father had seen us watching and was really upset. My brother said, "Now the police are going to come and blame me," because that boy's father was prejudice against him. Sure enough the police showed up. My brother asked me to back him up but I couldn't even remember being there. I didn't remember that incident until 15 years later.

I never really experienced life as far as feelings are concerned. I walked around in the world with my spirit not being totally connected to my body. As a result, when someone would ask me how I felt I couldn't tell them. If I went to the doctor and I was asked to describe the pain I was feeling, I could not tell him. He would ask if it was sharp or throbbing. I had no idea how it felt, sometimes I was not even sure if it was hurting. I remember once, I had hurt my foot. I thought it must have been broken because of the swelling. I walked to the doctor's office. He thought nothing was wrong with my foot because of my reaction. I felt almost no pain, it just hurt a little. He told me my foot was crushed – broken in at least six places. I asked him what I should do to look after it and walked home. This spilled over into all my senses, including taste. I could not say what anything tasted like. I just knew if I liked it. I disliked very few things. I later found out the only things I disliked were things I was allergic to or that disagreed with my system. I never really tasted anything. I only went by what my body needed.

My counsellor in the Sonhatsí:wa program taught me many different ways to control my dissociation. One of the things I was taught was meridian tapping.* Another easy thing I learned was to keep my feet literally firmly planted on the ground. Another was to press a couple of different pressure points on my body. This helped in the short term, or when I was unable to control it, but I still needed to learn to stop the dissociation before it began.

My counsellor worked with me to develop a plan to help me. The plan included my goals and different ways in which I wanted to accomplish them. The plan was a holistic plan that worked on my mind, body and spirit.

My counsellor helped me to release my anger and my

---

* Meridian tapping is another way of referring to EFT (Emotional Freedom Technique). For a brief explanation please refer to p. 205.

sadness through emotional release* sessions. She described the sessions to me before we started. At these sessions I was brought back to the actual incidents and asked to remember them and describe how I felt and let out any emotions I felt. I was really nervous and scared about this at first, and I was not totally convinced it would help me. My counsellor just asked that I try it. I was surprised at the results. I found I had a lot of sadness built up, sadness I would say that went right to the core of my soul. The sessions helped me to release this built up emotion. It took a few sessions, but it worked.

    My counsellor also worked with me to help build my self-confidence and my trust in other people. She encouraged and supported me in following my dreams. She helped me find my strength to say "No" and take control of my life. She encouraged me to join different therapeutic groups and I participated in an art therapy group that helped me on the path of getting my voice back. I also participated in a sexual abuse group where I learned I am not alone. I also learned to recognize signs of unhealthy relationships in my life.

    At this time, I realized one of my closest friends was very toxic to my soul. I believe everyone is equal and hate to see someone treated as if they are less than anyone else. We were on a vacation and my friend was saying very degrading things to the women of the country. I was very upset and disgusted by his behaviour and asked him to stop. I asked him several times, but he would not stop. By the end of the trip I had a breakdown. I called my counsellor as soon as I got home. She was able to work with me in a release session to help me get through this trauma. I knew I had been triggered by his prejudice treatment of women. I realized I could not be his friend anymore. Not only was he prejudice, but he also ignored my feelings and wishes when I asked him to stop. He could not see what was wrong. I have had to say goodbye to some old friends who were toxic to me, but I have been able to keep some who are positive and supportive as well as make new friends.

    My counsellor worked with me using EMDR* within our sessions. This is a session where I would just let my mind take

---

* Emotional release work, Psychodramatic Bodywork, p.203.
* EMDR (Eye Movement Desensitization and Reprocessing), see p. 204.

me where it wanted to go. I have had good results in solving problems and answering questions about myself. This helped me on my healing journey. It showed me things in a way I had not seen them before. It helped to join the adult and hurt child in me together.

One of the most important pieces for me to heal was my spirit. As a child I was very connected with mother earth and as an adult, I felt I had lost this connection. My counsellor used traditional healing methods and taught me traditional ways of healing I could use at home. This helped me a lot between the sessions. I became more involved with the community and attended some traditional teaching events. I also went on one of the community gatherings about the Great Law and the Peacemaker. This helped me to understand more about myself. It helped to heal my spirit. It helped to connect my spirit and my mind. Through these community events I have made a few new friends who also practice traditional ways. These friends have been very supportive and encouraging throughout my journey.

Today, I am a different woman. I am on my healing journey. I am self-confident. I have taken control of my life and I am making my own choices on how I want to live. I am following my dreams. I help others, but only if I can help without causing myself harm. I can actually say "No." I have learned to recognize when I am dissociating and how to bring myself back. I have also learned to recognize some of my triggers for dissociating. This helps me stop my dissociation in its tracks. If I do dissociate, it does not take me as long to come back. I can also recognize my feelings most of the time. This is wonderful, especially to feel pure joy. I am learning who I am. It is almost like I am a newborn child – looking at the sunrise for the first time. I feel as though I am experiencing a lot of things for the first time. I remember telling my counsellor about actually tasting chocolate for the first time; boy it was good. I am enjoying living.

I have been attending University part-time for a few years now, with plans to complete a degree. I never felt I was good enough to attend University before. It was very scary signing up for a class, but there were academic counsellors to help me. My first day of university was also very scary. I had picked a subject I was familiar with and I also knew the professor. This gave me a little comfort. After my first class I was all excited. It was not scary. It was just like attending high school. I knew I could do it. Throughout this whole experience my Sonhatsí:wa counsellor was there for me, offering encouragement and support. She also gave me names of people to contact for additional help with school related matters.

Now, I have good steady employment. I have learned to recognize good and bad relationships. I had a boss who was very toxic to me. I realized my spirit and self worth were being squashed. I recognized this right away and was able to look for another position. I have recovered from that experience a lot faster than I ever would have before. I am able to recognize other people's toxic behaviour right away. I am learning to avoid or counteract this type of behaviour. I am now in an excellent job with a great boss. I am still trying to build my self-confidence up with respect to the job but now I can recognize when there is a problem I need to address.

Today, I am also in a good, healthy relationship with a great, supportive partner. He looks after me just as much as I look after him. We are a team and we work together, sharing things together. I am glad we met each other now. He would not have been attracted to me before. I was too shy and self-conscious. I was like a scared cat. No one, that is unless they are someone who is not healthy themselves, would want to date anyone like that.

My life as it is today, would not exist as it does, if it were not for the help I received from Ganǫhkwásra[7]. I am a survivor of sexual abuse; I am no longer a victim. If you are a victim of sexual abuse, I encourage you to start your healing journey. If you do not find your path right away, do not give up. Everyone's path is different. I believe there is someone or a place that is the right fit for each and every one of us. If you know someone who is a victim or a survivor of sexual abuse, please be supportive of them. One of the most important things on a healing journey is good friends and family. It's funny how you start your healing journey and the right people are placed along your journey to help you. If you are a survivor of sexual abuse, I encourage you to continue your journey and when you are ready, share your healing with those who may benefit from it. I believe the most important aspect to healing is to have a holistic approach; encompassing the mind, body, heart and spirit. I believe people who are victims of sexual abuse need permanent healing, not just a band-aide. I do not believe this can be done without the holistic approach that is practiced at **Ganǫhkwásra'**.

Oh, and in case you were wondering. I can tell you all the names of the teachers I had in grade school and who my friends were. Healing helped me to recover a lot of my lost memories.

The Mirror's Answer

Sometimes it was hard to understand him.
He said I was beautiful,
And I didn't see it.
Sometimes his words I couldn't explain.
He said I was smart,
But what have I ever said?
Many times he's said I'm all he's ever wanted,
All he'll ever need,
But then I chose not to believe him instead.

Sometimes it's hard to be a woman,
When you look in the mirror,
And see nothing special at all.
Sometimes, to be a woman is scary.
Such a responsibility,
To hold day to day.
Many times he's looked at me like I'm heaven.
And I got afraid.
Then I asked him to look away.
One time I heard a wise one say this.
"Our women don't know how to be women."
Until now I didn't understand what she meant.
She said, "We've lost the essence of woman."
Through the years we've learned only,
The way to hide ourselves and forget.
I believe that what she said was the truth.
But the meaning I could not define,
Until I saw myself in the mirror one day,
Through my man's eyes.

Sometimes it's hard to understand him.
He says I'm beautiful,
But now I believe it.
Sometimes his words I can't explain.
He says I'm smart.
So then I remember all that I have said.

He tells me I'm all he'll ever want.
And so I ask myself, "Am I all I've ever wanted,
Or all I'll ever need?"
In the mirror I show myself the answer…
All that I am is a result of what I choose to believe.

K. Hill, June 13, 2003 "24"

Burn medicines that are for cleansing

Sage, cedar, sweetgrass and white pine are all medicines known to First Nations people that have the ability to cleanse; the air, our minds, our homes, our sacred objects. Burn one of them and let the smoke filter through the air or intentionally wave the smoke over yourself or the object you are cleansing. Ask the smoke to take away the negativity and carry your prayers for help and guidance to the Creator.

If you are not familiar with or do not have access to these medicines used by First Nations people you can use aromatherapy techniques to help calm your mind and spirit. These can also be used while you meditate or pray. Lavendar is well known for its calming and therapeutic effects. **Note:** Please check any precautions for using essential oils. For example, some are not recommended for use while pregnant, some are not to be inhaled directly and some should not be used at full strength.

"Today I am more who the Creator sent me to be"

What I remember about my early childhood is being with my mom and dad, brothers and sisters. I had people around me. I was the happiest kid. I had all the attention. My sister next to me is five years older. Then my youngest brother came but because he was so little I still had the attention. To me, I feel like I was really happy at that time.

The first time I felt violated in a sexual way was when I was four. My brother must have been about a year and a half. It was in the summertime. My sister used to bath us in one of those big wash tubs. She would fill it up and let us play in there because it would be hot. I remember jumping up and down and I didn't have any clothes on. I was just splashing around. I remember the freedom of doing that but that day when I was doing that this man was there. He was a friend of my mom's from when she and him were little kids. He wasn't really our uncle but that's what we called him. He was there and when I would jump out of the water I could see him looking at me, looking at my private parts. I remember jumping up a couple of times. When I first did it I saw him looking at me funny and I felt uneasy, it didn't feel right. Then I went back down in the water and I jumped up again. He was still looking like that and I felt worse. I did it again and there was just something about him that was different. Then I got down in the tub and I wouldn't get out. I just started shivering. My brother was still splashing and jumping up and down. My sister asked me what was wrong. I said, "He's looking at me." So she got a towel and went between him and me. She held the towel out and she picked me up. She carried me in the house and wiped me all off. She stayed in the house with me until I quit shaking but I kept shaking and shaking even after I had clothes on and it was summertime.

I still remember that shaking. After that happened, it was like my innocence was gone. The happiness I had before was just gone and I didn't want to be by myself with that man anymore. I guess at four years old I didn't know enough to tell people about it. My sister knew and when she would want to leave me in the house with my uncle I would say no. She always listened but I guess she never told anyone either. My mom would get him to baby-sit my brother and I. I always made sure my brother was with me all of the time. I would never let my uncle help me get dressed or help me do anything.

When I turned five the same man was still sexually abusive to me but in a verbal way. He would tell me what he was going to do with me when I got bigger and it was all sexual. Again, there was the fear, the shaking. I could feel it inside of my belly. I would just shake inside.

When I started going to school, I would try to be like the boys. At that time we used to have to wear dresses and skirts. I would always wear cut off pants underneath and I used to play with the boys. I would try to be a boy. I would play baseball and soccer and all of those things. I even talked how the boys talked. I was buddies with them.

When I was eight years old, this man came to our house and he was drunk. My mom let him in. My mom and my brother and my step-dad slept in the bedroom and I slept on the couch. The living-room and kitchen were all one room. So, I was sleeping on the couch and this man had gotten laid-out at the table. Later, I heard him moving around. I woke up and I was watching him. He started coming toward me and stumbling. He had the same look my uncle had. I looked at him and grabbed a pillow and put it in front of me. He tried to pull the pillow away and pull off my blankets. I just screamed for my mom. I was hollering and hollering for my mom. She came out and grabbed him. She pulled him and kicked him. She told him not to ever come back again. When he left my mom asked me if he hurt me and I told her no. She went back into the bedroom but I had that shaking again. I was just shaking and shaking. I had the blankets tight on me like I was really cold and I would just shake. After that I became really, really afraid of men, grown men.

The next year my mom went to work in the States but she left me and my little brother with my grandma. This time, it was my stepbrother who assaulted me. I heard him outside. I was upstairs at my grandma's house and I could hear him talking outside. He told these boys he was going to get into my pants. I was thinking about what he said and wondering what he meant. I didn't feel good about it because of how they sounded. I tried to keep my little brother with me but even with my little brother there my stepbrother tried to rape me. He grabbed my clothes. I used to wear dresses all of the time because that's what we had to wear to school. He grabbed my clothes and threw me on the couch and put his legs in between my legs. I told my brother to run over to my other grandma's house and tell her what he was doing. "Run as fast as you can," I said, "He's beating me up." I said he was beating me up but that's not what he was doing. So my brother ran and I kept fighting my stepbrother. I told him, "Gramma's coming! Gramma's coming!" Then I could hear her coming up the steps so my stepbrother took off out the other door. By the time she got there I was just shaking again like the other times. My gramma could see where my dress was ripped. I had marks under my arms where my dress had been pulling on me and I had scratch marks on my neck. She stayed with me until my other gramma got home. Then, my gramma sent for my mom to come and get us.

So it seemed like I was always afraid of men. It seemed like I was always getting sexually abused but not really. There was no penetration yet the threat was always there. Again, I wanted to be strong like a man so I would work really hard with my step-dad.

When I was nine, my mom and my sisters would talk about me getting a boyfriend. They would say, "Make sure you know how to wash dishes. You're going to be getting a boyfriend soon." I said, "No way am I going to get a boyfriend." That's when my eating disorder kicked in. I would eat and eat and eat to where I could hardly keep it down. Yet I would make myself keep it down because I wanted to be fat. I believed fat women didn't get boyfriends. I guess I learned that somewhere. So I kept eating and eating and I started gaining weight.

At school I would still be playing with the boys the same. We would still be like pals. When anyone would tease us, tease them or tease me, we would say, "She's my cousin," or "He's my cousin." It seemed like everyone would stop teasing us then. Even if we weren't related we would say that. I would always have that kind of friendship with them. It was like I would always be doing boy things so I could be like one of them. It was the same at home. I would work and help my step-dad do men things.

Then my uncle, the first guy who did the abusing, came back. He had been around now and again but he hadn't said anything. I would have this strength I would put out there. I used to think if he tried to do something I would fight him like how I fought my stepbrother. He started the verbal talk again, saying things like "You're getting older now. You're starting to have boobs. Pretty soon you'll have a boyfriend." Things like that. He would even say that when other people were around like my mom and others. They would laugh but I would see it in his eyes what he had told me when I was five. I remembered.

So I was always cautious. Then I started getting curious about it. What was that about? Why was he saying those things? We had a garage where he used to stay. There were two beds in there. My niece and I would stay in there sometimes but when he came back he would stay in there. One time he had gone and had an operation. When they brought him home, he asked me if I wanted to see where he had his operation. I didn't know. All I had heard was he had a hernia and I didn't know what that meant, so I said, "Yeah, okay." He took his pants off and he exposed himself to me. He asked me if I wanted to touch it. I said, "No, I better not." I could tell he was starting to get an erection. I said, "I'm going to go to sleep now." I just got in bed and went to sleep. He just went to sleep too. The next day he left. He got killed a couple of weeks later. I was happy and sad at the same time. I felt guilty because I was happy he was dead. I thought, "Now it's all over. It's gonna stop."

The next time I was sexually abused, I must have been twelve years old. I had stayed over night at one of my friend's house. This woman there sexually abused me while I was asleep because when I woke up that's what she was doing. I just felt disgusted. Then, there was the shaking again and wanting to fight. I couldn't understand. I had protected myself as best as I could against men. I had never expected a woman to do that. When she did that it was like I had no safety because now I was watching out for men and women. I began to not even trust my sisters and my mom. I just stayed away from them. I was just on-guard all of the time.

Then I went into a real bad depression. You can tell from pictures of me at that time, my hair and how I kept myself. I wore lots of clothes and I wouldn't wear a bra because I thought my boobs would show more. I would wear an undershirt and another shirt and a sweater and a jacket. I would always wear a jacket, even in the summer time. My hair was really straggly and in my face. I didn't really want to be seen. I wanted to be ugly so people would leave me alone.

I was only about twelve the first time a guy came to the house and wanted to take me out. I said, right in front of everybody, "Tell him to leave me alone and not ever come back here." He felt really trashed. I could see it in his face. He was a guy from school. I had befriended him just how I did with the other guys when I was younger. When I was friendly with him he must have taken it to mean something else. When I said that, I could tell I had hurt his feelings. It seemed like over the next year, there was another guy then another guy coming by, asking to take me out. I was big for my age. I was 5'6" when I was twelve and I must have weighed about 140lbs. I had breasts too so I looked older than I really was. Because of my behaviours, I also acted older so that's probably why those guys came there. At the time, I was thinking they just wanted to be sexual with me.

When I was about fourteen, my mom had moved in with my new step-dad. I stayed home with my youngest brother and my oldest brother and his family. We all lived in that house. I would baby-sit on the weekends to make money because I was in high school then. My brother drank a lot so there were always guys around. I would come home from school and chase them out. I would be really cross. I was afraid I'd have to fight because I didn't want to be abused. This one guy would tease me when I was being like that. He would be just hanging around but he was real kind to me. He would be the one to say to the other guys, "Let's go." He told me, "If I'm here and they start drinking while you're at school, I'll try to get them out before you get home." That happened a couple of times. I would be getting home from school and they would just be leaving. He would always be the last to leave and he would say, "Well, I tried to get them out." He would be nice to me like that so I started to look at him differently.

One day, this guy who had been so nice to me asked me to go out with him. I was thinking, "Okay, all of these guys were coming around here and it's probably part of life that I've got to get married some day. He's got a car and a job and he's good to me. Okay, I'll go with him." So I went with him. I never thought anything about it. He was twenty and I was fourteen when he and I started going together. I started living with him when I was fifteen. We had a baby when I was sixteen, got married when I was seventeen, then had another baby.

My husband was kind and he never forced me to do anything with him sexually. He seemed like a saviour to me because once I was with him I felt protected. The other guys quit coming around and nobody ever said anything to me or bothered me. I was always right with him. If we were around people that drank and someone tried to talk to me, he would say, "Leave her alone. She's with me." I felt really protected and safe with him.

It was when my kids were little, when my boys were about two and four when my sexual abuse stuff started coming back. I started going back into a depression and becoming suicidal. I was sleeping a lot too. I didn't know what was going on. The eating disorder started again too and that's when I really started gaining weight. My husband couldn't help me. He didn't know what was going on. I just got worse and worse. I couldn't understand how somebody could be sexually abusive to a little kid.

When my kids were small, I made them stay home. They couldn't go anywhere. They couldn't go and stay the night anywhere. I didn't want anything like that to happen to them. I became really over-protective and kept them home. I told them about abuse even when they were real little. I told them that no one has a right to touch their privates. I taught them how to take care of themselves when they were real little. I would give them a bath but I would get them to wash and dry that part of themselves. Thinking back now, maybe I made them ashamed, I'm not sure. I was so protective of that part of them.

Later, when my youngest brother went to a treatment centre, I was one of his support people. When I went there, I listened and I knew I had to go through there too. It wasn't just about drugs and alcohol. It was about why we use drugs and alcohol and overeat. So I went and I went just for me. I had never had counselling before then but once I went through that experience, I had to go and find a counsellor. When I started to go through my stuff, I got in a crisis situation. I phoned a friend who worked at Ganohkwásra' and she told me to go and see someone there. That's how I ended up at Ganohkwásra'. Before that, I didn't know anything about the organization.

Because of the sexual abuse I experienced, I suffered from anxiety attacks, acid reflux and ulcers. Yet, I hadn't told anyone in my family. I hadn't told anyone. I also had recollections of other family members being sexually abused by the same uncle who had abused me. I don't know if it was real or not but that's what I remembered. One day, I was having a really bad anxiety attack. My sister had to take me to the hospital. She asked me, "Why do you think that happens to you?" That's when I told her about the sexual abuse. Then I told my younger brother. Then I told my older brother. The last one of my siblings I told was my sister who was closest to me in age. I told her last because when I went into a treatment centre to help me deal with the emotional part of the abuse, she disowned me. When I had come back from the treatment centre she said it was a disgrace that I had gone there. She said I had put the family down. I told her she didn't know what I had dealt with and she said, "Well your problems aren't any worse than mine." I said, "Maybe not." Then I told her what I went through. My sister started crying. She said, "I didn't know. Why didn't you tell me?" I said, "Would you have been able to help me if I had told you? I'm telling you now so you'll understand why I went to treatment. I don't think it's a disgrace. I think it's a good thing because now I can live my life instead of thinking of committing suicide and running away. I can live. I did it so I can live, so my children can have a mother, and if I ever have any grandchildren, they can have a gramma. You can think and do whatever you want but that's why I did it. That's why I went there."

At one time I had three counsellors. I had one at Ganohkwásra', an addictions counsellor to help me deal with my eating disorder and a male counsellor because I had to deal with my male issues and my father issues. At that time, I needed support everyday, all of the time. So I was seeing my three counsellors once a week each, plus I went to 12 step programs. I went to ACOA meetings and AA meetings because I needed that much support. That's when my anxiety attacks were real bad and when I was having those shakes all of the time.

Once I started going through my healing there was a time when I felt like an "it". I didn't feel like I belonged anywhere. I didn't belong with the men because I wasn't a man and I didn't want to belong with the women because it was a woman who actually did the hands-on stuff to me. I didn't want to be a woman because I thought, "Women can do that? How could a woman do that?" I just felt disgusted and I began to gain weight again.

The weight is still something I struggle with. After my husband left, I lost sixty pounds in three months. I had weighed over 300 lbs. I had lost weight because I was fighting with trying to be alone and being so afraid. One day, I was walking along the street in Hamilton. I looked in a store window as I passed by. I thought it was someone else. I looked again and it was me. I was thinner. I got scared. I felt like I wanted to overeat again and gain the weight back.

I went back into a depression. All the shaking started again. I went to my doctor and I told him what was going on. He told me to go and see my counsellor. So I went to my counsellor and I had to work really hard not to go back into the eating disorder. It was my counsellor at Ganohkwásra' who helped with a lot of that.

I think what helped me a lot in my healing work at Ganohkwásra' was the release work.* The easiest thing to do was the hurt. I could let myself cry and feel that feeling move out of my chest. That was some of the first work I did. Then I got to the anger. I couldn't get angry before. I was so afraid of anger. I thought if I let myself get angry I would kill somebody. Ganohkwásra' was the safe environment I needed to be able to let myself become angry. Once I was able to do that, it helped with other things. It helped with the depression because my anger

---

* For a brief description of emotional release work refer to "Psychodramatic Bodywork" on p.203

wasn't going in anymore; it was coming out.

I couldn't get to my fear. I would just cover up. I'd slip into shame or hurt and I wouldn't go to the fear part. It was in a group I participated in at Ganǫhkwásra[7] that I first saw someone do a fear release. I heard the voice and I saw how the body shakes. Then I could feel my shaking. I was going through some things at the time where I would have the shaking but I was too afraid. I would just bundle myself up. When I saw another person do her fear work, I saw how she did it and she was good at it. I also saw what she looked like when she started and she looked better when she was done. I thought, "It works!" So then I was able to allow the fear to come for myself. Once I started letting the shaking come, all of the shaking I had since I was a little kid came. After I learned how to do a fear release, I stopped getting the anxiety attacks.

When I first started doing release work, I would only do one feeling in a session; anger, fear or sadness. Now I'm able to go through the whole thing. Sometimes I'll start with anger. I'll let the anger come but right underneath it may be loneliness then guilt, because I think, "Why am I lonely?" That's the unworthiness. Then the hurt would come and more loneliness. So I go through all of the feelings now. Finally, I'll get to a place of recognition. When I am able to recognize and accept the way things are, then the joy will come. Once I get to the acceptance part, the good feelings come because the negative feelings have gone out.

It used to take me a long time to do a session but now I can go through a major session within an hour. Before it would take me hours just to get to the feelings. Now I just let the feelings boil inside of me. I think about my safety because safety is the biggest thing for me. Then, once I'm there the sound will come. The counsellors would tell me to just feel the feeling then they would ask, "What does it sound like?" Sometimes it's like a deep growl. That's the anger. When it's fear, I can feel the fear. I just let my body shake and the sound come. When I do hurt, I feel it right from my heart. It's like it hurts and it has a different sound too. They're all different sounds. When I do shame work, I start retching like I'm going to throw up but it's really like a weepy, whining sound, hardly any sound.

What I learned at Ganohkwásra' was to get in touch with my feelings and deal with them in a positive way. One of the reasons I was afraid of dealing with my anger was because my anger was so huge. I was afraid I was going to hurt someone because I know our minds are really powerful. It was really important for me to learn how to identify my feelings and acknowledge what it feels like inside of me. The counsellors helped me to understand those things but I really learned the most in the art therapy group there. The facilitator would have clay or have us draw something and she would say, "What colour is your anger? What does it look like?" Once I started working with it I could identify it as a colour. Then a smell would come and I was able to get it outside of me. It was out there and I could see what it looked like. Then I would be able to get rid of it when I wanted to. When I thought of grief, it was black to me. Then it would go grey where it was surrounding me. It was stifling me. To be able to see that, identify, feel it and put it out there, was really something.

Sometimes when we worked on a piece in the art therapy group, I didn't want to get rid of it. For example, I kept my shame piece with me for the whole session. They asked me why I kept it. I said, "I have to wait. I'll get rid of it by the end of the session but I have to wait." At the end they came to me and asked why I kept it. I said, "Because I have to know what it looks like. I have to know what it feels like. It's been a part of me for so long it's hard for me to let it go. I need to know for sure that's what it is so I can get rid of it." Following my own instincts and what my own body told me helped me to own it because our feelings are our own. For me, I didn't want the feelings but they were there anyway. The art therapy helped me so much because I was able to hold it, see it, touch it, smell it. Once I was able to let it go, I was really able to let it go.

A sand tray exercise really helped me in my therapy. I couldn't understand how some people would think so differently in the same family. I would think, "How can they do that?" Then I did a sand tray. I was able to put everybody where they were in a particular scene. I was able to look at it from outside myself.

Once I saw where they were I was able to understand. I was able to accept what they were feeling because I was able to see everyone and how all the behaviours interacted. I was able to see how it affected everyone, not just me. And, I could see why their behaviours were the way they were then. That helped me to get outside of myself and to see what went on in my life. When I put it together and stood back I was able to process the feelings that came with it and it helped a lot.

A psychodrama[*] was what helped me to change some messages I held within me. It also helped me to see other people's perspective on things and take ownership of my own part in the dysfunction. I was able to look at what I was doing and understand that if I say certain things then of course someone is going to react to it. They're going to say something back. It was good for me to see it because it was being acted out. It wasn't just me feeling, it was other people too. I learned that my behaviour affects other people too. It's not a one-way street. Now I'm more able to take responsibility for my own behaviours.

When I think about Ganohkwásra[7], it's been a place where I've been able to learn about my feelings and express all of these feelings, no matter what they've been, in a safe environment so it doesn't hurt anyone else. It's a place that has been supportive in everything I've had to do, even as far as bringing in my medicines. They've always accommodated me. I think it's also been more than my one counsellor because when I did the psychodrama there were other staff members there who volunteered to help. For me, it was important for my health and well-being just to know they were there to help. Everything I needed to do, they were there to help me. Overall, I'd have to say the experience was life-saving because of where I was when I first went there and the different places I've been since, to where I am now.

When I know people who are in trouble with their emotions, I tell them there are places they can go to get help. I tell them they can go to Ganohkwásra[7]. I've found the counsellors are well trained and qualified even if that comes mostly from just working on their own healing. For me, I think if

---

[*] See Psychodramatic Bodywork on p. 203 for an explanation of this therapeutic technique.

a counsellor doesn't fit you then get another one. A lot of has to do with personalities. Everyone I've worked with has pretty good for me. Still, part of my adjusting was accepting other people and where they are. I think one of the biggest things I've learned going to Ganǫhkwásra⁷ has been that we're all human, even the counsellors. If one counsellor can't help you to get where you need to go, then there's others who may have a different approach or way of helping.

There did come a time when I thought I had most of my work done and I quit going to Ganǫhkwásra⁷. But later, I started having dreams of being raped when I was little and I knew I had to go back to counselling again to work specifically on the sexual assault part. This time I went to a counsellor in the sexual assault unit at Ganǫhkwásra⁷. I had to deal with all of the stuff that comes with that like being angry at my parents for not being there. My mom and dad both had to work but I was still mad at them. Even though my head understood why they had to work, they weren't there to protect me.

In my dream of being raped it seemed to me that it was when I was about six years old. I had all of the body memories of it. It was by a young man. He must have been maybe twelve years old. That didn't fit anybody in my family. The age difference didn't fit. I couldn't see the person's face in my dreams but I could see how his body was. I had all of the feelings of the tearing and penetration.

I was in school to learn how to be a social worker when that part came out. I had the people there that I needed. I went through my session right there with all my instructors and fellow students. The medicines were used and that's when I went to a different level. I went into the recall of when it really happened and when I was there, I called for my dad. In real life my dad didn't really help me but in the recall of it, he came and he helped me to stop the abuse. He pulled me out and he held me. I guess he did what I wanted him to do in real life. That really helped me. Then, when I thought about my dad, I thought, "If he had known, that's what he would have done." But he didn't know and I never told anybody about it.

I didn't remember that incident until I started dealing with sues. I had the body memories first. Then I had the feeling, the body feelings of it. Then ...rk I saw how and where it actually happened. It ... person who did that to me when we were living ...rms. That was a big healing part for me because ... when I would have a recollection, I would think of my dad... t would be like he was right there to help me go through whatever I needed to. Then the shaking part would go away.

That time at school wasn't the first time I had gotten to that level of spirituality but it was the first time I worked with the sexual abuse at that level. It took so long to get to that level with the sexual abuse because of the fear. That's one thing I didn't like. But, there were twenty-seven other people in there besides my instructors when I did that piece. I think it showed me I was at a different level; I could trust people with my story. Also, by then I had discovered about 98% of the people I had talked to had been sexually abused. They've experienced it in one way or another.

I have always come from a spiritual place when working on my healing. I think it's because I always pray. It tells us in our teachings that we're never meant to be alone. That's why we have those healing ceremonies. So, to me the spirit side has always been there whereas people can't always be there for us. My spiritual connections to creation are always there, to Mother Earth or Grandmother Moon. If Grandmother Moon isn't there then the trees are there or the sun or the wind. So there's always something. With people, we can't always have people and people die. I think the strength of my spirituality started with the **Ohędǫ́: Gaihwadéhgǫh**, the Opening Address. Everything they talk about in the Thanksgiving Address is a part of what we can use to heal ourselves.

For me, I don't see my spirituality as a separate technique in my healing. I go in with it and it's always there. Before I do any work I have to make everything safe. I'll smudge the whole area and everything that is going to be used. Then I take my tobacco and burn my tobacco and pray. I pray for the guardians to watch over me. I pray for them to make sure nothing bad happens to me because when I do my work it's like reliving those events. Then, if I am going to be working on anger I have about somebody, in my mind I will cover them in pink, unconditional love light so nothing is going to hurt them. Then I ask Creation to help me. With that I'm looking to the rain, the sun, the moon. I'll ask any spiritual helper to come and help me. Then I ask that the people who are there don't get hurt by what I am doing. Then, it's safe for me. At the end I smudge again and thank all of those helpers who came in to help me. I know it's more than my counsellor there. It's my helpers and their helpers plus creation. I think just trusting allows me to go where I go.

When there were suicidal times in my life, it didn't matter what I believed in. It didn't matter that I believed in Longhouse and suicide is against our way. None of that mattered. All that mattered was the pain I was in and trying to stop it. Feeling so unworthy and not belonging anywhere. That was the hardest time. That was a bad, suicidal time. My husband didn't even know I was like that. I never really told anybody. I was well into my healing before I would admit it to any person who wasn't a doctor or a counsellor.

I always went to the Longhouse. I always did the dances, helped out, whatever. When I was going through the time when I was fainting and I was sick all of the time, my mom would go and get her fortune told and I would have to have feasts. But, I think what really brought me back to my spirituality was when I started going to AA meetings. When I was doing that twelve steps they would remind me to think, "I can't. He can … If I let him." The first three steps are admitting we're powerless over something. That's how I was. I was powerless over what was happening to me because I didn't understand it. I couldn't do it but there was a power greater than me that could and I had to let him do it. I had to let him help. That coincided with my teachings from the Longhouse, my beliefs to pray to the Creator. Before then, all my prayers were at the Longhouse, asking for the crops to grow, thanking the Creator and watching them burn tobacco. I didn't really use it personally. Once I started going to AA and I started hearing them talk about a higher power and praying for help, I started praying to **Shǫgwayadihsǫ**h to help me. I prayed to the guardians to help me because when I listened to our opening I was reminded about the four guardians who watch over us and help our minds.

When I was dealing with my sexual abuse there was a time when I had called a disease to me, when I had actually said I wanted my vagina or uterus to just be gone. I felt that being a woman was the cause of my sexual abuse. I had that thought when I brought a sickness into my body, then I had dreams about it. In the dream I had this disease and it smelled really bad, like the disease was rotting the inside of me. I woke up the next day and I told my sister. She said, "You better go to the doctor." So I did go to the doctor and he did a pap smear. When it came back it was positive, I had cancerous cells. I went home, told my mom and she said, "You know the medicine for that. Take care of it right now." So I started taking my medicine and when the next full moon came I made a fire, went outside and prayed. I said, "That's not what I meant. I didn't mean for me to get cancer or for me to die. It was just because of the pain." I prayed. I sat there at the fire with my tobacco and I prayed. I acknowledged what happened and that I had hoped for that disease. Then I talked to the moon and the Mother Earth. I told them I was sorry and I prayed for forgiveness. I just totally surrendered myself to them. When I went back to the doctor those cells were still there but I kept praying to the moon every month and after a year the cancer cells were gone.

That's when I started going to moon ceremonies and having moon ceremonies because in our belief the moon works with the women for our monthly cycle. I had to talk to her because I couldn't talk to anyone, not my mother or my sisters. So, I talked to the moon. I asked for forgiveness and was able to forgive myself for what I had caused, what I had brought into my body. I worked really hard and once I got to a place of forgiveness I felt worthy to live. I used the medicines I have. I used that to help me get better. Finally, my tests were clear of the pre-cancer cells and now I have been clear for five years.

Once I started talking with the moon, my femininity came back. I started to feel that it is okay to be female and I made my connection to Mother Earth, to the Skywoman and Grandma

Moon. I saw other things in our teachings, in our culture, that are put there to help us heal and I used those things to help me to get where I am today. The healing ceremonies helped me to grieve and lift the grief of my lost childhood, my lost teenage-hood, my lost marriage and my lost children.

Today, it seems to me the last part is to lose weight. As soon as I start losing weight it's as though I want to sabotage it. I still do that. I don't know what it would be like if I were thin. It feels like if I got thin I would lose my strength somehow because I still associate the overweight-ness, the extra armour, with strength. I don't know what I'm afraid of but I think I'm afraid of being abused. I guess in one part of my mind I think being overweight worked for me. I know if I lose weight now, I'll go into a depressing spiral yet I have to be able to go through that process. Everything is in place for me to do that now. My doctor said I have a standing prescription for anti-depressants. He said if I ever need them I can go and get them. I know where to go for counselling and I know I have a real strong support system. I can reach out to someone if I'm going into a spiral because I know that's what will happen.

I also know I have to keep healing. I wanted to heal so my kids weren't affected by it and so my grandchildren aren't affected by it. I know the more I stifle myself, the more over-protective I am, it's going to affect them. Still, I told my boys my story. I tell them all of the time to watch their kids. I tell them to teach them early to protect themselves and be aware of who they have babysitting. I told them all of that because no child should have to go through what I went through. I did my best to protect my children and I want them to do their best to protect their children. I have strong feelings about that. I know if I was ever abused again or if anyone ever abused my grandchildren, I would fight verbally, physically, legally. It doesn't matter who it is.

Today, I help others who have been sexually abused. I help them go through their work so they are able to live a better life. I've used our ceremonies to help them. I've used the repentance to help them find self-forgiveness and to forgive others. I have forgiven all of my abusers because I know they too were victims. They were victims of somebody who did that to them and they were sick people. I guess it's more about forgiving ourselves, because I think as a sexually abused person there is always that thinking of "What did I do?" That's where the forgiveness has to come in. If you think, "I smiled at them, I didn't stop them, or it felt good and I just let them do it." There's guilt so the forgiveness has to come. If someone carries that guilt I help them with it. I tell them it's normal because it's a natural feeling and it's normal to want to feel good and we can forgive ourselves for not having the learning to stop, to know it was unhealthy and it was going to effect us longitudinally, especially if we were little. We use tobacco. We'll put the tobacco down or we'll burn it or sometimes they write letters first to get out all of the negative stuff like calling themselves down. I work with them and then we'll burn the letter with the tobacco. The tobacco then becomes the healer.

I've had to do work on self-forgiveness when I brought that sickness into my body. I had to forgive myself for being angry at my parents for something they had no control over at the time because they didn't know it was happening. I had guilt about that. The adult person understood but the little one didn't. I had to do a lot of self-forgiveness. Every time I felt I was bad, that I did something wrong, I would do work on forgiveness. Even when I felt like I was bad because I was happy my uncle got killed, I had to do self-forgiveness work. Every time I got to a place where I felt like "I'm bad," I did a self-forgiveness piece around it so I could feel like I was worthy to be alive, so that I would realize I'm not a bad person.

Today everything is different. Now, I want to live. Now, I can be a woman. It's okay for me to be a woman and I know how to fight against an abuser. I work with young girls, youth. I always talk to them about keeping themselves sacred, to have boundaries and to be respectful of other people's boundaries too. I guess I have learned what I have so I can share that with the young people. Today, I'm more who the Creator sent me to be, more than I have ever been.

Nya:weh Shǫgwayadísǫh

Forgiveness

Long time ago, an elder told me,
"Alcohol is poisonous, so is hate.
You must let go of it, before it's too late."

I asked her, "How do I do that?"
She said, "You need to pray.
You must be nice, starting today."

At eighteen years and full of anger,
There was no way I could even like them;
Those who hurt me now or then.

But that old woman whom I loved so much,
Taught me the truth about changing myself,
Taught me to love myself, to move forward without looking behind.

Elders are truthful and wise.
When they speak of forgiveness
It's the only way we can let go of those lies.

Forgiveness is what lights our way.
Don't give up; just give it to
The Creator in the sky.

D. Harris

Have a sea salt bath

Sea salt holds the natural healing properties of nature to cleanse and restore. It can also rid you of negativity and protect you against it. While holding a pinch of sea salt in the palm of your hand give thanks to the Creator for giving us this healing element . Gently drop it into your bath water. A pinch of sea salt in your bath will help cleanse your mind, body and spirit of negativity as well as protect you from it.

"I hope it never has to happen to someone else"

My story begins in the summer of my eighteenth year. I was a virgin, still attending high school. This was when I met Mark*. He was a couple of years older than me but there was a mutual attraction. We flirted and eventually exchanged phone numbers. Within a month, I had a date to hang out with Mark and his friends. A couple of Mark's female friends approached me about him. They didn't come out and say anything directly but it was insinuated that Mark was the "welcoming committee" for many young women who were new to their circle. What they were saying about him didn't bother me at first. I thought they were just teasing me because they were his friends.

We saw each other a few times over the next couple of weeks. One evening, we ended up making out and were naked in my bed. He wanted to have sex but I told him I wasn't ready. I was a virgin and I wasn't ready to give that up. We had made out and taken our clothes off once before and that's as far as things had ever went. Everything was consensual up until then, but then he made the decision to force himself on me. I tried pushing him away. I told him no, I told him I wasn't ready and I didn't want to lose my virginity. It seemed like hours had passed. I kept telling myself it wasn't happening, it wasn't real. But I could feel the pain; that part was real. When he finished he casually got up, got dressed and left, as if nothing happened. I was curled up in my bed and in shock. I felt dirty, used and worthless. I put some PJs on, curled up and cried myself to sleep.

When I awoke the next morning I felt disoriented and still in shock. Somehow, I managed to drive to a clinic to get checked out and get the morning after pill. I didn't feel together anymore. My body and mind were going through the motions of these activities but I felt numb. I kept telling myself it never happened. While at the clinic, I was asked a series of routine questions. I remember the nurse telling me what happened was called date rape. She asked if I wanted to press charges. I said, "No." I didn't think I had been raped. Rape was a brutal thing – ripped clothes, bruises, injuries, etc. Rape was when a man stalked you, followed you until you were alone in the dark, by your car or walking home. That never happened to me. I let this guy in my house, and I let him in my room. He didn't break in. Hell, I even

---

* Mark is not the actual name of the perpetrator.

let him take off my clothes. I didn't have any bruises or injuries from the force. My head was pushed into the bars of my headboard and he forced my legs apart but he never threatened to kill me if I told. He didn't even have a gun or a knife. He didn't hit me either so I thought it couldn't have been rape. After the assault I began feeling all sorts of emotions at the same time—sadness, emptiness, shock, guilt, anger. I knew he had done something wrong but I couldn't acknowledge it and I didn't want to label it, otherwise I would have had to admit to myself that it was real.

About a week after the assault I confronted him. I asked him, "Do you know what you did to me?" He casually said, "Yeah, I forced you into it." I let him know how upset I was about the whole incident. He told me he was sorry for what he had done. I don't know what was going through my mind then but that seemed to be okay for the time being because I wasn't afraid of him. I didn't feel he was going to try anything again. Maybe because it wasn't violent or what I thought or pictured a rape to be. Still, I was scared, not of him but because he ejaculated in me, meaning I could have been pregnant. Fortunately, it turned out I wasn't pregnant.

The possibility of a pregnancy was really something for me to think about. I wanted to make sure I was prepared for any result. I wanted to make sure I was making a rational decision with a (somewhat) clear head. I contemplated the worst case scenarios and what I would do. I didn't want to find myself in a situation and make a decision I would later regret. I knew I didn't want anything to do with Mark; I didn't want him to be involved in any way. I knew if I was pregnant I would have the child. Adoption would be an option because I didn't believe in abortion. It was my religious background that had me thinking that way. I believed it wasn't my decision to take a life. But, I also wondered if I could love a kid who was the result of a rape. The irony of this situation was I am the result of my biological dad raping my mom. The same thing had happened to her but she got pregnant. That's how I was conceived and I've always felt like she's resented me because I am a constant reminder of her assault. I couldn't bare to put another generation through what I went through. It wasn't fair.

I hadn't told anyone except a couple of close friends. Eventually, my mom started questioning me because I was really emotional and I would cry myself to sleep. She kept asking me and asking me until finally I blurted out, "I was assaulted." She got really upset and she told my grandparents. It was very emotional.

In the fall, I returned to high school. I took time to think everything over. I decided I wanted Mark to take responsibility for the mess he caused in my life. I thought maybe if I filed a police report, a judge would find him guilty, put him on probation and make him get counselling so he wouldn't do it to someone else. At first I really didn't want to file anything because I didn't think people would believe me and I didn't want the whole reserve to know. Regardless, I went to a nearby town and tried to file charges. But, because the assault never happened in that town, I was sent back to the reserve to file a report. It was really difficult and scary but I felt it needed to be done. After speaking with the police, I became scared because Mark was going to find out I had told the police. I didn't know anything about the whole legal process. I didn't know what I was getting myself into.

When I filed the report I had to tell the story of what happened. I had to tell everything, every little detail. I had to tell it first to a police officer and a second time in front of a video camera in an interview room. I had to tell it to the Crown Attorney even though he had watched the video and read the police report. The Crown had to ensure I was telling the truth and that I told the same story each time. When I had to recount the activities of that night yet again, I detached from my emotions so I wouldn't relive the pain over again too. I pretended I was just telling someone else's assault story. I know now that I was dissociating; my mind wasn't feeling what my body was experiencing.

I also started attending an anxiety and depression group. I was also seeing a counsellor, trying to deal with the depression. I purchased a new bedroom set. I didn't want to see or be in my bedroom or bed any longer. I wanted to get rid of everything because that's where it had all happened.

When he was finally arrested, the police had him in custody for twenty-four hours. The officer told me that he was asked for his side of the story but he didn't say anything. By law, he didn't have to. Whenever there was something new going on in the case, the police officer I was working with would call and update me. He was very supportive. I had a lot more contact with him than I did with the Crown Attorney. When I had to meet with the Crown Attorney, the officer would also meet me there. The Crown Attorney approached me differently than the officer. He was very professional and not as understanding. He wasn't disrespectful but it was clear this was just a job for him. He was definitely not there for emotional support.

I was missing a lot of school because I was going to counselling, then I was going to group, and then I was going to meet with the police and the Crown. There was a lot of additional stuff going on outside of school. It was starting to get really hard for me so in January I quit school. I couldn't take it anymore. I couldn't concentrate. I was a big mess.

There were a lot of times I needed to talk to someone and it would be two o'clock in the morning. I was just a mess. I got a number for a help line and I talked to that person on the phone. They set up a phone call and a meeting. I started seeing a counsellor who dealt specifically with sexual assault. With my counsellor, I talked about everything that had happened. I told her how I was feeling and when the trial was coming up she gave me handouts and different material I could read. We would discuss what was going to be happening. She tried to prepare me for just about everything.

It was a year after the assault, before the trial actually took place. I don't know how long it lasted throughout the day, but it was a day long. I was really anxious and scared. I had my support people with me; people who loved and believed me. My counsellor was also there as well as a few of her co-workers and two placement students. They met me in the parking lot. My counsellor explained to me why it was important to have so many people with me. They created a barrier around me so Mark, or the people who were with him, couldn't say anything directly to me. It was to help me feel safe. It helped but his mom was saying things off to the side, rude things. I just blocked her out and kept walking. All of my support people sat with me until it was time to go in. Then, we all sat in one row except my mom and step-dad, they sat at the very back. His girlfriend was the only person sitting behind him.

Mark was questioned first. He seemed very calm when he was on the stand. I was so frustrated because his side of the story had changed. I was crying, whispering, "That's not true," every time he told a lie. I was really upset with his version of events. He distorted the truth and said we had consensual sex. He brought up that I was on medication for anxiety and depression more than once. I couldn't understand what my being on medication after the assault had to do with what happened. He presented himself as a hard-working, good guy who was innocent.

When I was called to the stand, I didn't feel as nervous as I thought I would. I felt like I was prepared for what would happen. The counsellor told me about different tactics the lawyer might use to try and cause me to feel like I had done something wrong. She pretty much prepared me for how his lawyer would treat me like crap. While I was on the stand, I just kept looking at my counsellor. I didn't really look at anyone else. It was like I was just talking to her. I didn't want to look at him at all. My counsellor had told me to take my time and if I needed a glass of water, I was allowed that. They had offered me water so I took it.

His lawyer was just shooting questions at me and I was answering them if I could. He wanted specific dates and times but with the time span that had gone by, I could only answer, "I don't know. I don't remember or I'm not sure." I had kept a journal where I had written down dates but I didn't know I could refer to it on the stand. I tried to take my time so everything was clear and his lawyer wouldn't get me to stumble or be able to put words into my mouth, yet he still was able to do that. I got frustrated and asked him if I could finish what I was saying. He just said, "No, that will be fine." Every time I tried to finish what I was saying or say, "I'm not done," he would just say, "That's fine," and went on to the next question.

When the Crown questioned me, it was a lot more

comfortable for me. I knew the questions he was going to ask me ahead of time. He took his time and gave me time to respond. It was almost like he was guiding me through to what the next question was going to be so I didn't have to sit and think about it for a long time. Overall, he was pretty good about things. While we were in the trial, I was writing questions on napkins and passing them to him and he was really good about answering them. I was asking questions about what was going on or what things meant. He would write on the napkins and pass them back.

The only other witness questioned was the police officer who was working on my case. What the defence really concentrated on was that I hadn't told the police officer this one part of what happened when I first made the report. My friend was with me at the time and it wasn't something I wanted to talk about in great detail with him there. I told the officer about it later when I had to tell my story over again, as well as when I was recorded and when I talked to the Crown. Mark's lawyer asked the officer, "Why isn't this part in the initial report filed? Did she tell you about this part?" The officer said, "No, she didn't tell me in the initial report but she did tell me at all of the other interviews." The lawyer asked, "Why didn't she tell you this part at the very initial meeting you had?"

Although it was very frustrating, I thought the trial had gone okay. I knew the circumstances; it was a "he said, she said" case and a fifty-fifty chance of finding Mark guilty. I didn't want it to happen to someone else. My rationale for going through with the trial was that Mark would think twice before trying it again. During the waiting process, I had found out about other victims, none of who were raped but experienced Mark's attempts. I tried to get those girls to come forward so the Judge would know Mark had tried it before and probably would again. It really hurt to know that and yet no one would come forward.

When the verdict was read, I cried. I was pretty angry. I felt like crap. I felt like no one believed me and I was betrayed by the justice system which was supposed to protect me and other women in society. The Judge found Mark not guilty. He said he didn't want to ruin Mark's life. Mark had a good job and no previous record. The Judge also used my virginity against me.

During the trial, he had asked if they could question me about my sexual status. Legally, the court can't ask those types of questions but I felt I had nothing to hide. He ended up using that against me. He concluded that I was really confused and created a scenario where I had sex then changed my mind and wanted to take it back. I thought that was a ridiculous conclusion. Why would I go through months and months of having to tell my story over and over again, and just having to deal with this whole trial, only because I changed my mind about having sex?

The trial caused me nothing but ill feelings towards the justice system and the government because they created the laws. The Judge created a scenario of his own. I had let Mark into my house; I let him into my room; I let him get undressed; I undressed and we were in my bed. So that combined insinuates consensual sex? I didn't have a right to say "no," to stop things when I became uncomfortable? I battled my court experience for a very long time. I felt those people should have protected me. They should have done something. I don't believe justice was served. I wasn't respected there as a person. From that experience, I still don't have any faith in the legal system, the government, the police or anything having to do with authority. I don't trust them.

After the trial, I thought it would have been easier if I had been in some sort of denial instead of it being an actual rape. Had it been consensual and a situation where I just didn't want to believe it, I think that scenario would have been easier to deal with. I felt like I was going crazy. There was constant questioning, constant analyzing and breaking everything down over and over again. I would go over everything in my head and question my actions. There were some warning signs, why didn't I do anything about them? Why didn't I recognize them? Why didn't I listen to other people?

When the trial was held I had just started college. Having that going on started off my years at college pretty bad. Going to college is something really big to begin with. Being away from home and my family for the first time meant I had a lot of freedom. Yet, I wasn't making the best choices for myself and that made it even worse. I pretty much went downhill. I didn't care about myself or school. I changed from the person I was before it all happened.

Before meeting Mark, I was optimistic and naïve. I attended church regularly. I hung out with all different types of friends. We would go to the movie theatre or rent movies a lot. There was really only one guy I had dated. I met him in grade ten and dated him off and on through high school. He was my best friend.

I was an average student in school. I rarely skipped. I had a pretty close bond with a couple of teachers. One of my teachers was a counsellor and he got me into his peer helping class because he felt I would be appropriate. I was doing peer mediations and going to peer-helping conferences. I didn't drink and I didn't do drugs. I didn't smoke. I don't think I even swore. A lot of people said I was a goody-goody.

After the assault I stopped going to church. To this day, I have not returned to attend church services. I felt like I had been a good person. I respected my elders and did as I was told so what had I done to deserve this?

As for school, I started college but was skipping classes a lot. When I didn't attend I was sleeping and when I did go, I went in my pajamas. Other students do that too so it didn't seem like anything was out of the ordinary. I would just grab whatever was on the floor, clean or not. I lived right across from the school so that was good but I was forgetting the whole reason I was there.

I couldn't concentrate on my studies. I started partying Tuesdays, Thursdays, Fridays and Saturdays. I started smoking. I started smoking pot. I tried ecstasy. Being high was my break from thinking about what had happened and thinking about how I was not doing the greatest in school. The drugs provided me with that relief and I felt like I was actually able to forget everything and have some fun. I was laughing, just being free. I didn't have to keep analyzing everything and feeling like crap.

I also became promiscuous. I didn't care who I slept with just that it was my decision. I was taking back my power to make the decision about having sex and who I would have sex with. My rationale was that I wasn't a virgin anymore; my no sex until marriage rule was thrown out the window. I was rebelling against God's commandments for letting me down. Before I had even met Mark, I believed being a virgin was really sacred. It really meant a lot to me and I was really proud because that was rare. I felt like I was pure. I had made my mistakes but I liked and accepted who I was. The rape had torn my essence and affected all aspects of my life. It clouded over me everyday and haunted me, even when I slept. I felt dirty and I just lost respect for myself. My self-esteem really took a nose dive too.

My depression began taking over my life. My family wasn't there to help me through the hard times. After the trial I don't think it was ever mentioned again. I didn't feel I was getting a whole lot of emotional support from them and they didn't try to understand what I was going through. I no longer had the support of my best friend either. He was going to college somewhere else and slowly stopped speaking with me. I would call him and try to reach out for help. It hurt because I felt very alone and eventually I stopped caring about life.

I would spend days at a time in bed. I would only get up to eat and use the bathroom. Sometimes I would shower, change my pajamas and go back to bed. I didn't really care about my future anymore. Many times, I thought about killing myself. I didn't feel life was worth living anymore. I actually tried to commit suicide numerous times, taking a lot of pills, cutting my arm and slowing trying to get to my wrist but I couldn't do it. I dropped my course load to part-time the second term because I began to fail. I couldn't go anywhere or do anything. If I did go out, it was just to ruin my body and contaminate my body with drugs and alcohol because it took away the pain, even if it was only temporarily. I put myself in dangerous situations, which resulted in a second assault later that fall.

I didn't want to return to the reserve because I knew he was there. I didn't think it was right that he wasn't held accountable. I kept reminding myself that the whole reason I had gone through with the trial was so it wouldn't happen to other girls. When I did go home strangers were approaching me and asking me if I was crazy. That was the rumour. He was telling people I was crazy. I had already felt like I was going crazy, then people were asking me if I was crazy. So many things were going through my head. I didn't know what to do. I didn't have any supports around me. It was really hard.

When I returned to the reserve for summer break, I was assaulted again but I was passed out. Two days after, I ended up in the hospital for overdosing on tranquilizers. I had talked to a friend on the phone and she knew something was wrong because I was slurring my words. When she came over, she saw the bottle and it was empty. She saw a couple of pills on the floor so she took me to the hospital right away. They made me drink this black, chalking-like substance and they had to call my mom. This one nurse asked me why I would do something so stupid. I couldn't believe she was talking to me like that when it should have been obvious that I was already feeling pretty low. I don't think I was really trying to kill myself. I think I just wanted to rest. I just wanted to be free of the pain for a little while, to just sleep and not have to deal with all the rumours and everything that was going wrong.

I still hadn't coped with the rape. I thought I had coped with it because I was able to tell my story. But now I know I hadn't forgiven myself for it. I had tried seeking help from various counsellors. I saw many professionals but I didn't connect with them, and they didn't seem to get my description of the reserve atmosphere or how people responded to my claims. I wanted to talk to somebody who was familiar with the environment of an Aboriginal community because I felt maybe they would understand my situation a little more. Maybe they would understand how the rumours affected me, and how people who didn't know me approached me and asked if I was crazy. That's when I went to get an intake done at Ganohkwásra'. Once I completed the intake, I was put on a waiting list and then I was set up with a counsellor in the sexual assault program.

I was comfortable telling my counsellor my story. It felt good to just have someone to talk to. I knew she was listening and she wasn't judging me. She guided me to explore and understand my feelings and issues. She provided me with insight and coping techniques. I believe I was meant to meet her; she would assist me on my healing journey. I believe having a counsellor from an Aboriginal background definitely helped too. She understood the dynamics of the reserve. My counsellor was able to empathize and I didn't feel alone anymore. I finally had found a person who understood what I was talking about. While I was going to college, I was only able to see her once a month but there were other times I was able to increase my sessions to once a week.

The big turning point for me was to accept and forgive myself. I had put my health and well-being through a lot after the assault and the trial. I had even blamed myself for the assault. After a particular group session, I left deep in thought and I carried this negative feeling home with me. Once I arrived home, I made a list of all the thoughts I had running through my mind. I didn't want to forget anything so that I could talk to my counsellor about it in our next individual session. When I left that session, I felt such a big relief and I literally couldn't stop smiling. It felt like a weight of guilt had been lifted off my shoulders. That's when I knew I had forgiven myself. I could say, "It wasn't my fault" and honestly believe it. I don't hate or hold a grudge against Mark but that doesn't mean I forgive him either. I felt I needed to let it go, otherwise it would have eaten me away inside. I just hope it never has to happen to someone else.

As for living in the same community, I don't see him and I'm thankful for that. I don't know how I would feel or react to seeing him. I don't think any rape victim is able to put this sort of thing behind them a hundred per cent. The past may be in the past but it still hurts and saddens me when I look back at that time in my life. I can watch the news or read about assault and/or abuse and it still touches me. Mark and the rape don't disrupt my thoughts like they used to. At one point, every aspect of my life and my relationships were wounded. Today, I've taken back so many pieces of myself that were stolen.

Participating in the Level I and Level II groups for sexual assault survivors at Ganọhkwásra' helped considerably. I learned a lot of different coping and healing techniques: Reiki, release work, tapping, quantum touch, breathing exercises, visualization.* The level one group wasn't as awkward as I thought it would be. I automatically gave 100% to the group

---

* For a brief description of these techniques please refer to p. 203-206.

because I desperately wanted my life back. It was the second group that challenged me to look further within myself and really grow as a woman.

The Level II Sexual Assault Survivor's Group was an art and play therapy group. I love doing art and crafts so I jumped at the chance to join. This group permitted us to explore and express ourselves through different means of communication. There was one group session which started off with one of the facilitators reading an article from a local newspaper. We heard about how some members of the community reacted to a young female who had come forward about a sexual assault. Once the facilitator was finished reading we were asked to take a piece of clay and express what we felt. The degree of comfort I felt with my group members, sparked openness and creativity. My artwork was another confirmation that I was growing and changing. It was a really unique and beautiful experience.

The women in group each contributed something very real and unique. Honour, knowledge, wisdom and experience was shared along with culture, inspiration and understanding. The group provided me with the kind of support I needed and would not have found any other place. The group consisted of women of various ages, with different beliefs and lifestyles, but we shared a common experience. My sisters and I came together to find resolution and to walk part of our journey together.

My knowledge of abuse and its effects has also expanded. I can apply a lot of what I have learned to my chosen field. At times there were topics in group I couldn't relate to but it was information I can use to help others. I've also learned different, healthy coping techniques that will help me both personally and professionally.

If a sexual assault survivor looking for advice approached me today, I would suggest getting a rape kit done immediately. Even if you decide not to report or press charges immediately, you will have hard evidence for later. Something to remember is that the legal process is not for everyone. The statistics are low regarding the number of sexual assault perpetrators found guilty. My case took a year to go to court but the trial process can go from months to years. I didn't feel the justice system helped me put any closure to my experience. It made me feel victimized all over again. I wouldn't encourage anyone or deter anyone from pressing charges. I would just caution that it's better to know what you're up against before proceeding.

For me, the legal system changed nothing. I was still a victim and putting Mark in jail wouldn't have taken away the memories or the issues the rape created. It's been years since it happened. Yet, I'm determined to continue growing and learning. I stopped questioning myself about the "what-ifs" and started dealing with present day issues. I've just accepted the things I cannot change and I work on what I can change—me. My goal is to one day love myself again because I'm worthy of love.

What I need from you...

Please don't tell me what I shouldn't have done or said
I do that to myself every day within my own head

What I need is someone who won't blame me
For a wrong that was done that I couldn't foresee

Something that only he and I can truly know
Responsibility he twists so his part does not show

Lies that are said to leave me with blame
Desperately trying to be rid of the shame

My wounded community members who gossip galore
Getting a sick high off of one's blood, guts and gore

That night my soul was mangled, twisted and torn
Which left me with so many hazy moments to mourn

Mother and Father still love me I ask
Just hold me and tell me this pain will not last

You raised a good person, no one can take that away
And no matter what happens by my side please always stay

Brothers who sit uncomfortable, and no longer know what to say
Please remind me that someday, his action he will pay

Sisters wake up, I need to hear your voice
Help me to tell them it all depends on choice

I fight to be heard and so the truth can be known
Exposing the trauma of rape so the pattern is shown

Maybe someday there will no longer be such a large range
Of perpetrators having more rights than victims, I hope that will change

Who am I you ask as this comes to an end
I leave you with one final thought I must send

Go in the next room and you'll find me in there
Sound asleep holding my little brown teddy bear
I am your own child, the one that you hold
At night you cover up so I won't get cold
You stay up rocking me when I'm sick with the flu
You encourage me everyday as I try to tie my shoe
I make your day with my giggle and smile
Enjoy my innocence, it's here only for a while
Chances are so high that I will be the victim of rape
By someone I know and trust—my soul that will shape
But you can make such a difference in this trauma you see
All I want most of all is to know you BELIEVE ME!

Anonymous

Sing or Chant.

Singing or chanting will calm your mind. It takes our thoughts away from what is troubling us as we concentrate on the words, rhythms and sounds. This causes us to experience a calming, relaxing effect, taking the negativity from our minds, bodies and spirits through the vibration of sound.

"No one is going to stop me from living my life"

I was brutally attacked and sexually assaulted. I thought I was going to die and that was the worst feeling I have ever felt in my life. I ran for help and the police were called. My attacker was caught shortly after. I still can't believe this happened to me. I know things like this do happen in the world but I never thought it would happen in my community and especially not to me. I couldn't believe someone could be so sick and heartless. That event has had such a tremendous impact on my life.

Before the attack, my partner and I had been separated for a couple of years. My children and I lived by ourselves. We had become comfortable with our new lifestyle. I worked and they went to school. We had a pretty consistent routine from day to day. It was nice.

I had been in counselling at **Ganohkwásra'** in the women's program for a couple of years. I was having marital problems so I came to work through that. Actually, my partner had gone first, then I went to deal with what was going on with him. So really, my intention for going was to help my partner, and not for me. Then I found out that's not how it works. They said, "We're not here to talk about him at all." I kept going and he quit so we just grew farther apart. I wanted to move ahead and learn how to resolve things but he was stuck in the same place.

I had learned a lot in women's counselling. I learned how to do release work.* That was really hard. I couldn't find my voice for a long time but I think things had built up in me for so long that I had to do something. Finally, I just told myself if I wanted to keep moving forward because I had to do this. I know I grew a lot as a person in that time. I don't think I could have ever gotten through the attack without having been the person I had become because of my counselling at **Ganohkwásra'**. It helped me to stay focused, to not lose it. I had to be aware of my surroundings. I had to keep thinking. If I had went blank, I don't know what could have happened.

Ganohkwásra' was a big support after the attack. A couple of the counsellors came over right after it happened. They weren't only there for the emotional support either. They brought food and helped out however they could. I couldn't stay in my house because I was so afraid to be alone so they were going to

---

* For a brief description of emotional release work refer to "Psychodramatic Bodywork" on p.203

let me stay in the Next Step Housing, but I ended up moving in with family. They also helped me to get hooked up with the ALERT system to help me feel safe. It's a button you wear around your neck that works through your phone. It's connected directly to the police station so if you push it the police will call right away. If you don't answer they'll just come. Everything I needed to feel safe, **Ganǫhkwásra'** was there to help me with.

After the attack I began to see one of the counsellors in the sexual assault program. She also referred me to see a therapist in Hamilton who specialized in the Emotional Freedom Technique (EFT), the tapping.* She explained to me that this technique would help take the trauma from my immediate memory and put it in a different part of my brain so when I thought about it, it wouldn't be as traumatizing. I would tap on different parts of my body while I talked about the attack. I think this helped a lot. I started seeing her about two weeks after the attack so it was still fresh for me. The tapping, along with the work I did with my sexual assault counsellor at **Ganǫhkwásra'** and the traditional healing I did on my own, really got me through that most difficult time.

I continued to go to **Ganǫhkwásra'** for about a year after that. They really supported me throughout the whole court process. I met with the Transitional Support Worker because he knew about the legal process. He helped me to prepare for the preliminary hearing. He told me about some of the things that might happen in court and some of the things that might be said. We had a little court proceeding to help me practice speaking about that horrible night in my life. That helped too. I was able to say what I had to in front of people I trusted instead of just going to the court and saying it for the first time in front of strangers.

At the preliminary hearing I had to disclose the specifics of the attack in detail. That was very difficult for me. It was very stressful and I had a lot of anxiety. Seeing my attacker and talking about what he did to me sexually, in front of him, his family and my family was very difficult and brought up feelings of shame, anger and guilt. I tried to keep as calm as I could before the hearing. I had a lot of support from family and friends

---

* Refer to Emotional Freedom Technique on p. 205.

that day. My sexual assault counsellor had taught me to use a technique to keep me calm, by touching a certain part of my arm. All of the preparation I did before the hearing was very helpful.

The Crown Attorney first asked me questions about what had occurred. That was compared to my statement given in the police report. He helped me to feel as comfortable as possible considering the specific details I had to give, and that I had to point out my attacker in the court room. I was very angry at him and wished him dead. I used that anger to tell what he did to me so he would be embarrassed for being a sick person. I also had to look at pictures of myself taken the day of the attack. It was difficult to see what I had looked like. It looked like someone else instead of me. Then I was questioned by the defence counsel. I know I had an attitude toward him because I knew he was going to ask me questions that would try to help his client. His questioning did not take long and I felt more confident after he was finished. The Judge commented that I was a very brave person for handling the attack they way I did and for attending the hearing.

After the hearing, I met with my counsellor and I just broke down. I let my guard down and released all my feelings of anger and shame. My attacker had pleaded guilty and I was so glad I did not have to attend a trial.

At the last court date, the statement I gave at the preliminary hearing was read in court as well as my victim impact statement. Friends and family were in attendance for support. It was difficult to hear all the details of the attack again, especially in front of my family. The details were also published in a local paper and I felt violated all over. I didn't want people to look at me and think about certain details or judge me by my actions.

Since the attack, my life, and that of my children, changed so much. I was unable to look after my children the way they needed me to. I couldn't physically look after them for a few weeks, and emotionally, I was unable to for months. I did the best I could. I was unable to stay alone when I returned home, so I had family members stay with me every night. My children's routine had changed so much that they started to act out. They would have some really difficult periods. They were also very afraid the man might come back. I tried to assure them and they were in counselling for a bit too.

I had a difficult time sleeping. I would stay up late until I was very tired and then I would be awake early in the morning. I struggled with thoughts of why this happened to me. Why did he do this to me? I often wondered if it would happen again.

I was unable to work for a number of months after the attack. I was having difficulties concentrating and I was going over the attack many times in my mind. What if things turned out differently? What if I had been killed? I struggled with thoughts of "Did I bring this on myself? Did I ask for it?" I think about having died and at times I wished I had died. I even contemplated suicide. That's how bad it got. There were so many things that happened to me that night. I was brutally beaten and raped. That is a lot for one person to handle physically, emotionally and mentally. I was somewhat detached from my feelings right after the attack and felt numb. Later, I began to feel the trauma to my body and spirit.

A few months after the attack, I returned to work but for only a short time. With thoughts of a possible trial and also thoughts of my attacker being out of jail in a short number of years, I was constantly upset and I had a hard time concentrating. I decided to leave work until after the sentencing date.

Before the attack, I was comfortable being in public. I could go out with friends and feel at ease. That changed dramatically. I was unable to go to public places in the community. I tried to go to my niece's graduation shortly after the attack, but I was unable to stay as the feelings of anxiety and fear were overwhelming. I felt that people were staring at me, thinking about what happened to me and judging me. Over time, these feelings have changed and I am relatively at ease in public again. Today, I understand that maybe people just didn't know what to say. I am proud of my community. It can be very supportive when something tragic happens. I received cards and flowers as well as monetary gifts from several community members. I am very grateful for all the support I received and I believe our community is fortunate to have the services **Ganǫhkwásra'** provides.

That whole thing was so very hard for me. But, I just kept thinking, "I don't want to feel like this. I can't just keep thinking about it and being a victim." So I kept up with my counselling and I did whatever was suggested or whatever I thought I could do. I just did it. It was hard but I wanted it to be gone. Otherwise, I wouldn't be able to be around here, in this community.

I did a lot of release work in my sessions shortly after the attack. I had to do it right away because it was just too overwhelming. What was bothering me a lot was that it was publicized in the local papers. The second time it was in the paper after I had the hearing, some of the things I had said in my statement were released and published. Then, the Crown Attorney was informing me of what might happen in terms of my attacker's sentence. He gave me examples where the attacks were similar and the sentence was only two or three years. That bothered me too. I didn't know what was going to happen.

After the final court date, I ended my counselling at Ganǫhkwásra[7]. My counsellor suggested I join a group but I decided against it. I felt that going there and continuing to talk about it was just bringing up stuff more. It was keeping me in that place of being traumatized by it. I just had to quit going so I could go on with my life and stop thinking and talking about it.

Still, I know I'm not done my counselling. Maybe, for now, I'm taking a break. When my attacker gets out I know it will be difficult for me and I'll probably need that support again. For right now, he's not around and I feel safer knowing he can't hurt me or anyone else where he is. I just don't have to think about it all of the time. I can go on with my life. It's not that I don't think about it but I can't let it control my life. No one is going to stop me from living my life.

With counselling I learned it was not my fault. I did not ask for this to happen. No one deserves such a horrible thing to happen to them. No one has the right to put another human being through that!

Now, I have to just think of all the things I do have. Today is so different from the way things used to be. I have a new partner and he's really good to me. I quit drinking and he doesn't drink either. That makes such a big difference. It's just such a different life. Sometimes I think getting into this relationship happened quick, and I'm surprised I was able to do it but I just figured I'll go along with things and what's meant to happen, will happen. We were friends first so I think it was just a matter of building trust with him. I had to do a lot of work around men in general. That included people I knew, strangers, anyone; just men in general. I wasn't comfortable being alone with anyone, not even my relatives. The work with my sexual assault counsellor helped; tapping, release work, art therapy. I had to get that trust of men back for myself. It just took time.

I also have to trust that everything happens for a reason. I have to think that way about the attack too, for my own sanity. I didn't think anything good could have come from such a horrifying experience but my life has totally turned around. The way things happened, I think I wouldn't have the good life and loving family I have today if it hadn't happened this way.

For anyone who has experienced a similar sexual assault, don't let yourself continue to be the victim of your attack. Your attacker may have taken and hurt your body but they can't control your mind or your feelings. Don't give them the power to stop you from experiencing life for the rest of your days on this earth. Also, reach out. There are other people who have survived similar horrifying experiences. Talk to them and know you are not alone. Finally, do any traditional ceremonies and medicines that are suggested to you. They really do help. The power in our traditional ways, in our people, is amazing.

For community, if you know someone who has been sexually assaulted, don't stare, don't judge. They have been violated and traumatized enough without having to be subjected to gossip and criticism. If you don't know what to say, perhaps try smiling and saying, "I was thinking of you. I'm glad you're here." It helps to know people care.

The Monster Under My Bed

One night a monster
From under my bed
Who answered to the name of "Dad"
Stole my childhood from me.
I was horrified and defenseless.
My childhood was never the same.
I miss my childhood.

He watched my every move.
He would do harm to me and my family if I told.
So I remained in the shadows, terrified and untrusting.
Every night I cried myself to sleep … No one helped me.
As the years passed, Mom still went to BINGO
And left me home with the monster.

Attacked by the monster every night while no one was home.
The monster walked around in the day and everyone trusted and liked him.
But no one actually saw the real monster underneath.
My world was distorted and turned upside down.
Walking with a big ball and chain wrapped around my ankle.
Eventually I became numb to the pain.

I got stronger, angrier and more disgusted.
I learned that this monster really had no power.
Every day I took a tiny bit back.
Then one day the Police knocked on my door and asked me what the monster did to me and for how long.
Strangely, I remembered each day like it was yesterday.

Finally the monster was put into a cage.
Now it was the monster who gets watched and controlled.
His freedom has been taken away so he can't hurt me anymore.

But I realized a part of him was inside of me.
I was petrified.
Nine months later, it was over.
In order to protect her, she went to live with a family where she

would have two older brothers and be safe from the monster forever.

Today I'm rebuilding my life.
Now I have a husband and a healthy family surrounding me.
Three beautiful children for whom I would lay my life down in order to protect.
Every night I look under my children's bed for monsters
So they and I can sleep at ease.

G. Miller, 2004

Have someone comb your hair

Our hair often holds the thoughts, feelings and emotions of our mind. Combing your hair while relaxing the mind and consciously thinking good thoughts, will help to strip away the grief you may be carrying in your hair. Having someone else comb your hair for you can help even more, as it gives you the extra nurturance many of us often do not get enough of throughout our lives.

Ganǫhkwásra' Family Assault Support Services

Family violence challenges our most deeply-held values about family, relationships, responsibilities and the importance of the family to our survival as First Nations. We want to intervene, but we don't want to interfere. We want to protect our men, women, youth and children, but we're reluctant to put our people into the hands of the mainstream justice system. We want to stop the fighting and hurting, but we don't want to break up families.

Because of the seriousness of these dilemmas, we try not to believe people we love are enduring or inflicting pain and suffering. Despite our concern for our families and community, our ambivalence keeps us silent about family violence. And because those who abuse and those who are abused share our values and these dilemmas, they too keep silent. In this way, we remain isolated from one another, unaware of our mutual concern and unaware of the extent of family violence within our community. Our people suffer in silence, and the violence infects first one generation and then the next – for children learn what they live.

For mainstream, Western society the battered women's movement in Canada began well over thirty years ago. At Six Nations of the Grand River, the movement to address family violence in our community began in 1986. Concerned community members began to meet about family violence. Initially, the concern was for battered women and their children. For some years, members of our community had been sheltering women and children who fled from violence in their homes. From this experience, they came to understand the fear and life-threatening danger in confronting an abusive spouse; and they came to understand how services outside our community often compounded the fear and isolation of our women and children who were being abused.

Rallied by the late Wilma General, a group consisting of Reva Bomberry, Alice Bomberry, and Shirley Farmer took their concerns to the Six Nations Band Council. This small group of women were later joined by Joanna Bedard, Dorothy Russell and Belva Monture. With the endorsement of Band Council they formed the **Ganǫhkwásra'** Steering Committee. The job of this committee was to develop services for battered women and to seek funding to develop and operate a program.

A comprehensive study was then undertaken by the Steering Committee in the summer of 1987. Phase I of the project determined how many women in our community were being abused or were at risk of being abused. It also determined how many children in our community were living in violent homes and/or were at risk of being abused. Phase II of the project designed a program to address the needs of the Six Nations community in relation to family violence services from the philosophical base of our culture and values.

Utilizing the results of the feasibility study, the Board of Directors and staff, in consultation with a local management consulting firm, BomCor Associates, were able to develop a mission statement for the organization. This mission statement is as follows:

> "To provide, through a non-profit, charitable organization, for the maintenance, stabilization, revitalization, and enhancement of the Iroquoian family structure in a culturally sensitive manner."

As well, the project completed a community consultation process which resulted in the development of a plan for service implementation including community education, outreach services and community service development.

From its conception, **Ganohkwásra'** has responded to the community's needs. The initial priority was safe housing, with a vision to create a place where women could learn how to be strong again and take their rightful place within our community as leaders. Community "outreach" counselling was identified as a need that could be addressed prior to the completion of the shelter. In 1988, the steering committee accessed and was guaranteed funding to provide community outreach counselling to women impacted by family violence. It was at this time that the dreams and visions of the founding members were becoming a reality. Shortly thereafter, the community began to ask, "What about men?" A research project was then undertaken, enabling **Ganohkwásra'** to begin providing counselling and support to male victims and/or perpetrators of abuse in 1991.

With financial assistance from the Canada Mortgage and

Housing Corporation as well as the Province of Ontario, construction of a residential shelter commenced in the fall of 1991. At first, some community members felt this building should be located in an unknown, hidden location. However, the Ganǫhkwásra⁷ Steering Committee was determined to have the shelter built in a prominent location so the community would be forced to recognize the impact family violence has on our people. Ganǫhkwásra⁷ was built, and continues to stand, in the village of Ohsweken, on Chiefswood Road, in the centre of our community services and business sector.

During this development phase, it was identified that there was a severe shortage of housing for women who wanted to remain in the community after fleeing from an abusive relationship. Again, Ganǫhkwásra⁷ responded to this need. In 1994, funding was secured to build eight second stage housing units. In 1996, financial resources were obtained to construct an addition to the shelter, specifically to house and expand the existing men's program. In 2001, the Six Nations/New Credit Youth Lodge was added to Ganǫhkwásra⁷ residential services. The Youth Lodge has been in existence since 1993 under the direction of Six Nations Elected Council. The original vision then grew to include the entire family, recognizing that everyone has their roles and responsibilities in a healthy family unit.

Today, Ganǫhkwásra⁷ provides holistic programs to men, women, youth and children. Our services for men set Ganǫhkwásra⁷ apart from any other family violence organization in Canada. This is another example of how the brave women who comprised the founding Board of Directors, as well as the Director of the organization, focused on the needs of the community and our values of family. They recognized that every person (men, women, youth and children) has the potential to be abusive or a victim of abuse. We continue to recognize this today, as the organization works towards the stabilization, maintenance, revitalization and enhancement of individuals for the restoration of family units through residential services, community counselling services, transitional support services, community education and volunteer programs.

The implementation of all services is based upon the

philosophy behind the name of the organization. **Ganǫhkwásra'** is a phrase in the Cayuga language meaning "love among us." It was the name chosen for the Family Violence Program at Six Nations early in planning to express our purpose and philosophy in creating a community-based program for victims of family violence. It conveys an attitude of community support and hope for families wrought with violence, and it implies a sense of community responsibility for peace among all our members. **Ganǫhkwásra'** is the goal we seek for every member of our community, and it is the methodology through which we work to attain that goal.

"Love among us" is more than a feeling or emotion, it implies active participation in living together in peace and harmony. The Great Law* has given us teachings of peace, strength and the good mind which is ultimately attained through **Ganǫhkwásra'**, love among the people. It must be understood that love, as it is spoken of here, is not the intimate feelings experienced between a man and a woman, nor is it the feelings of caring we have for our loved ones. Love, in this sense, is a great love for the people. It is believing in our connectedness with each other and with all of creation. It is understanding that whatever we do will affect somebody or something, even if it's years down the road. This is why we must always be thinking of the seven generations to come. This is how far love must extend.

Love is also doing. It is cooking for a family who has lost a loved one or has just been blessed with a new baby; it is listening to the grief of a friend with a broken heart; it is visiting for no reason at all; it is offering food and drink to guests in your home. This kind of love is accomplished through commitment, respect and the use of a good mind.

Working to continually develop and maintain a good mind takes conscious efforts on a daily basis. This means always looking for the positive in every situation. It means that when life puts barriers in your path, you must use the strength of your mind to make that situation positive. To have a good mind, we must also live a life without the influence of drugs and alcohol, gambling and gossiping. We must treat people with love and give thanks everyday to the Creator for life, to our protectors for their protection and to creation for continuing to be there for us. It can be difficult to keep a good mind as life will test us. However, we must remember if we try our best everyday to strive for it, our whole being (mind, body and spirit) will be more healthy and happy. As well, if we each aim to have a good mind we will see the positive effect it has on our families, Clans, Nations and our Confederacy of Nations.

Strength comes with the practice of a good mind and the peace that comes from the love among the people. The power is there when we practice our ability to work together at all levels, everyday. Then, in situations of crisis we all work together to come up with solutions knowing that what we do or say now is going to have an effect on those unborn. The power must extend just as far as the love.

These Onkwehonwe teachings integrate the mind, body and spirit. At **Ganǫhkwásra'** they are combined with mainstream counselling techniques to provide a basis for helping one to accept responsibility for their total being. Our counsellors are trained in a variety of therapeutic techniques. Although every counsellor may not possess a working ability in all techniques, they call on each other for assistance when working with individuals or groups therefore all program participants at **Ganǫhkwásra'** are offered the same opportunity to experience these techniques. The following are the techniques used at **Ganǫhkwásra'** with a brief explanation of each.

Individual sessions
One-on-one counselling sessions provide individuals with education about issues of family violence and sexual assault. These sessions also enable individuals to explore, express and vent their emotions. As this is occurring, individuals are also encouraged to do "present day repair work" on their past traumas. This reclaiming and reparative process may involve practicing within sessions to speak up to someone who is emotionally controlling to them; or practicing how to express self in a good way rather than aggressively.

Groups

All programs offered at Ganohkwásra⁷ provide their participants with an opportunity to experience healing within a group setting. Currently community counselling programs offer a level one and a level two group. Most often the level 1 group is an educationally focused therapeutic group while the level 2 group is a therapeutic group where members will do their healing work within the group setting. When needed, a level 1.5 group is offered to those participants who are beyond the education stage yet not quite ready for the intensity of a level 2 group.

Groups are also offered specifically for survivors of sexual assault. The level 1 group for sexual assault survivors is an educational and preparation group while the level 2 group is an art and play therapy group. Art and play therapy provide a safe and gentle way to work with healing from sexual traumas. Ganohkwásra⁷ recognizes that most organizations do not support healing from sexual assault in a group setting; however, it has been our experience that these groups have had amazing results for participants. Group members are able to re-build trusting relationships with each other which is fundamental to their healing process, trust being one of the main violations experienced by sexual assault survivors.

Psychodramatic Bodywork®

Many Ganohkwásra⁷ staff members are qualified, or are in the process of being trained and certified, in Psychodramatic Bodywork®. There are two parts to this work; intense emotional release work and psychodramas.

Intense emotional release work offers individuals a safe method of expressing intense feelings of anger, fear and sadness associated with experienced trauma.

Psychodramas are an extremely reparative, role-playing technique. Psychodramas provide a safe containment for individuals to re-enact, vent and reclaim their own personal power from a past trauma within their lives. Staff members are chose for roles and given lines to speak by the participant (or protagonist). Individuals are directed to address their feelings to these characters in a safe therapeutic environment. With this technique, individuals are challenged to take on the perspective of the other characters involved, enabling them to gain a wider perspective beyond their own, as well as gain new insight into their role and responsibility to self. New approaches to a situation may also be practiced. Further perspectives are offered as the staff members de-role and explore their own experience with the role they played, as well as insights to playing that particular role.

For More Information Contact:
Susan Aaron Workshops
www.youremotions.com
Tel: (416) 699-3211
Email: aaron@youremotions.com

Eye Movement Desensitization and Reprocessing (EMDR)

EMDR is an excellent, trauma-specific technique that offers our participants an opportunity to connect to their spirit, re-visit an experienced trauma or examine a current issue and "see" the reparative piece that needs to occur. Integrating traditional approaches with this technique, the worker guides the participants towards resolution.

For More Information Contact:
Sue Frazer
519-884-1029
www.frasercounselling.com
Email: sue@frasercounselling.com

Reiki

Reiki is the channelling of healing energies of the universe. It is used with individuals to release energy build-ups or blocks in their bodies that have formed as a result of physical disease, chronic pain, old injuries, accidents, repressed trauma and emotions.

For More Information Contact:
Jane Burning and Michelle Thomas
Universal Energy
Tel: (519) 445-1904
Email: universalenergytlc@hotmail.com

Emotional Freedom Technique (EFT or tapping)
EFT involves tapping on meridian points throughout the body. Energy tapping will calm an individual, preventing severe abreactions such as panic attacks or high blood pressure which may occur by revisiting an experienced trauma. It can also be used to identify blocks, change behaviours and negative thinking patterns as well as help people with such things as weight loss and allergies. At Ganohkwásra' we like to think of tapping as an acknowledgement of the thoughts and feelings we are holding in order to release the negative energy we are attracting to ourselves as a result. This approach makes the technique more culturally appropriate as many of our ceremonies are about acknowledging spirits, energy or "what's there" and helping them to move on.

For More Information Contact:
Nina Bregman's Energy Therapies
http://members.rogers.com/ninabregman/
Tel: (416) 423-7831
Email: ninabregman@rogers.com

Shiatsu
Shiatsu is a hands-on technique using the fingers and palms of the hand to apply pressure to particular points on the body to correct imbalances in the body and enhance its natural ability to heal.

For More Information Contact:
Wholistic Therapies and Training Academy
Website: www.secretwestwoods.ca
Tel: (905) 659-2806
Email: hmgleave@aol.com or hmgleave@attcanada.ca

Choice Theory and Reality Therapy
Together, these counselling techniques help people to reconnect in their meaningful relationships. They are based on the power to choose healthy behaviours in relation to self and others.

For More Information Contact:
Jim Montagnes
Tel: (416) 261-1085
Website: www.makechoices.com
Email: jmontagnes@makechoices.com

Other Therapeutic Techniques
Art and play therapy techniques, as well as grounding techniques, prayer, meditation and visualization exercises are also utilized in assisting individuals with their healing work.

For More Information Contact:
Art and Play Therapy Techniques
Betty Bidard-Bidwell
519-524-2852

All of the techniques used at **Ganohkwásra'** can be considered energy work and therefore compliment the spiritual teachings of First Nations culture very well. Each technique is rarely used in isolation. Our counsellors have developed their skills to work with energy to a point where they can employ a number of energy techniques into one session.

Because our unique healing approach is so successful, more and more people are looking to **Ganohkwásra'** for help. **Ganohkwásra'** has been a model for other First Nations communities looking to establish community shelters and crisis services. We've had visitors from First Nations communities in the U.S. and across Canada from the Blackfoot Nation in Alberta to Innu from Davis Inlet, and have travelled as far as New Delhi, India. Thus, the Community Education program has proven to be instrumental in carrying our message of **Ganohkwásra'** (love among us) throughout our community and beyond. Becoming aware of family violence issues and wanting change is the first step to healing for many individuals. Over the years,

Ganǫhkwásra' has consistently provided the community with opportunities to increase their awareness of family violence and sexual assault, learn about cultural history and beliefs, and honour individuals who have made positive contributions to creating love within our community with such community events as "Acknowledgment Night" and "Children's Day."

Ganǫhkwásra' has also developed a unique First Nations specific training on Family Violence Prevention for staff and volunteers of Ganǫhkwásra' as well as for other professionals and interested community members. This training is known to have a waiting list of up to a year. It differs from other Family Violence Prevention Training models in that it is presented with a First Nations approach, providing a unique perspective on these troubling issues.

In 1999, Ganǫhkwásra' was acknowledged for its exceptional work with individuals and families when the Six Nations community was awarded the Ontario Trillium Foundation's Caring Community Award. The foundation characterized Ganǫhkwásra' as "the jewel of our community as it works with the whole family – women, men and children, to achieve emotional healing and united families." The Trillium Foundation is an agency of the Ministry of Citizenship, Culture and Recreation.

Since 1986, Ganǫhkwásra' Family Assault Support Services has evolved into a successful, professionally operated community service. We are extremely proud of the accomplishments we have made over the years. We acknowledge the healing power and availability of mainstream services in nearby communities, especially during our earlier years when we could not meet all of the needs of our people. Today, we offer our community members unique, creative and spiritually-based services. We will continue to move ahead and help our people heal from the traumas of family violence and sexual assault, right here in our own community. It is our goal to enable families to find strength and support in the values and customs of First Nations people. It is through Ganǫhkwásra' (love among us) that we can put an end to family violence. Everything we need is there for us in our original teachings, in our original way of being.

Ganǫhkwásra⁷ Programs and Services

Residential Services
Etiya'takenhas (Oneida word meaning "We Are Helping Them")—Shelter
The shelter program provides stablization through a safe, homelike atmosphere 24 hours a day, 7 days a week, for individuals who are seeking safety from abuse and violence.

Gayęnawáhsra⁷ (Cayuga word meaning "Helping Ourselves")—Next Step Housing
The Gayęnawáhsra⁷ program is for individuals who choose to live independently and violence free. Gayęnawáhsra⁷ offers services for maintenance, revitalization and enhancement for single parent families in safe, temporary housing.

Tsi Tionkwatention A'non:wara Rason:ne (Mohawk word meaning "My Home On Turtle Island")—Youth Lodge
The Youth Lodge is a six bed co-ed residence for youth ages 12-18 experiencing serious difficulties in their lives.

Community Counselling Services
Counselling Services are available for women, youth, children and men who have been abused, at risk for abuse, and/or are abusive. Abusive behaviours and their generational sources are explored in a caring, non-judgmental way. The commitment to this holistic healing process may be long term, based on the needs of the individual.

Ah sęh sa wa:dǫh (Onondaga word meaning "A New Beginning")—Women's Program
Gaǫdwiyá:noh (Cayuga word meaning "They Take Care of Children")—Child and Youth Program
Sahó'nikonrí:io'ne (Mohawk word meaning "His Mind, Body, and Spirit Has Been Healed")—Men's Program
Sonhatsíwa (Mohawk word meaning "Your True Self")—Sexual Assault Program

Transitional Support Services
Ge hé ẹ gọ yẹ na:wá's (Onondaga word meaning "Helping You to Straighten Out Your Life")
The Transitional Support Worker provides supportive, individual long and short term transitional planning, safety planning, advocacy and referral services to individuals who are seeking violence free lives and a holistic well being.

Community Education
Ag gwa dẹ́h ye:s dah nih (Seneca word meaning "We Are Teaching Them")
The Community Education Program staff are available to inform the community of Ganọhkwásra' programs and services, the dynamics of family violence, related topics and effects on individuals, families and communities in a culturally sensitive manner. This is achieved through facility tours, presentations, workshops, seminars, conferences, media ads and interviews, distribution of resource materials, brochures, posters and newsletters. There is also an on-site research library.

Volunteer Program
Kayethẹka:rya'ks (Tuscarora word meaning "They Volunteer")
Volunteers are an integral part of our organization. Through the support of volunteers we are able to expand our services to our participants. Volunteers are utilized for driving, fitness supervision, child and youth groups, research, fundraising, childcare, library services, public relations and special event. Volunteers receive extensive training so they can gain a better understanding of family violence and the effects it has on individuals, families and communities. Through caring and sharing volunteers become more understanding and capable of helping themselves and others to grow. Volunteers at Ganọhkwásra' gain wisdom and compassion as well as skills, confidence and friends.

Sonhatsí:wa

Sonhatsí:wa (Your True Self) is the name of the sexual assault program at Ganohkwásra⁷ Family Assault Support Services. It was the dream of the organization, the Director and the Board that we would help members of our community do their healing work around the issue of sexual assault. It is an issue that has affected the lives of so many of our people. Ganohkwásra⁷ had been working with family violence for a long time but when it came to sexual assault we were referring our clients to non-Native therapists outside of Six Nations.

Since sexual assault counselling was an important gap within our community, Ganohkwásra⁷ took the lead role and began to organize conferences and workshops focused on sexual assault education. While this was providing our community with much needed education and understanding about sexual assault, these were not forums for people to complete the healing work they required.

Fortunately, in 2000 the Aboriginal Healing Foundation put out a call for proposals. The purpose of the Aboriginal Healing Foundation was to encourage and support Aboriginal people in building and reinforcing healing processes that address the legacy of physical and sexual abuse in the residential school system, including intergenerational impacts such as family violence, abuse, incest, sexual assault, neglect, alcohol and suicide.

It was no surprise to the staff of Ganohkwásra⁷ that many of the current traumas and socio-economic challenges within our community were directly linked to the impact the Residential School system has had on our people. The Aboriginal Healing Foundation was a positive acknowledgement that the government was finally recognizing that the Residential Schools did violate First Nations people mentally, emotionally, physically and spiritually. Furthermore, the Foundation was providing an opportunity for First Nations communities to become a pro-active part of healing from these traumas. Therefore, Ganohkwásra⁷ submitted a proposal and in November 2000, Sonhatsí:wa opened its doors to a list of community members wanting individual sexual assault counselling.

Since that time, Sonhatsí:wa has worked to meet the

demands of community members, initially by providing one-on-one counselling and later adding groups for sexual assault survivors.

RESIDENTIAL SCHOOLS

Residential schools were instruments for assimilation and Christianization, implemented by the federal government and various Christian institutions. The first residential school opened in 1804 in the United States. In Canada, the schools were in operation from 1804-1984. The churches were given the responsibilities of running the institutions, as well as providing some financial assistance, while the federal government determined the policy under which they would operate as well as contributing financially and conducting inspections.

The Mohawk Institute Residential School was located in Brantford, Ontario, approximately 20 kilometres from the Six Nations community. This institution was a joint effort between the federal government and the New England Company (NEC) to civilize and convert the Six Nations people. The NEC was a protestant missionary society. The missionaries they employed at the institute were all Anglican members of the Church of England. The Mohawk Institute (known by community members as the "Mush Hole" for its reputation of serving oatmeal for breakfast, lunch and supper) began as a day school in 1828. Programs were expanded and in 1834 rooms were added to board the students; at this time, it began operating as a residential school until it closed in 1970.

Sonhatsí:wa has been conducting a Residential School Survivor Survey with the sexual assault program participants. Each participant is asked to complete a questionnaire upon intake. This survey differentiates between who is a residential school survivor or an intergenerational residential school survivor (family member of a residential school survivor). The survey also identifies when it is not applicable to the participant. As of 2004, of the total number of participants who completed the survey, all but three Native participants listed themselves as being impacted by the residential school system. The residential school survivors were able to relay their memories and experiences of attending the residential school, while the intergenerational residential school survivors conveyed their understanding of the effect that the Mohawk Institute has had on their lives; a direct result of having family members attend the school.

All Residential School Survivors surveyed attended the Mohawk Institute Residential School and were admitted into the school before age 10. Each individual stayed within the school for a minimum two years. All were taken to live at the residential school as a solution to social assistance or poverty – "My parents could not afford to keep us when we were kids." When asked about the traumas they were exposed to within the residential school all participants conveyed the sense of abandonment they experienced from parents and siblings. Some noted that although their siblings were also in the residential school, they were forbidden to talk with them as the children were segregated into groups. All participants discussed memories of being severely beaten and strapped for a variety of reasons or reasons unknown. When asked if they think about the residential school experiences today, most responded that they did not like to think about that time in their lives. One participant acknowledged the nightmares she continues to have to this day from living in the school as a child. When asked how this experience has affected them today, all discussed their own inability to give to others emotionally. One participant described herself as an "emotionally absent parent." All had hopes and a heart-felt longing to heal their wounded inner child in order to feel safe today as an adult.

It is well known, at least in First Nations communities, that survivors of the residential school system have experienced insurmountable losses including culture and language as well as a First Nations' understanding of our families and the world around us. The losses experienced by those who attended the Mohawk Institute have been passed down through generations as survivors re-integrated into society, having families of their own and subsequently raising their children without the languages, traditional parenting skills, expressions of love or cultural identity. From there, the legacy of the residential school continued as their children then grew and had children as well. Because family members of the residential school survivors are also affected by the residential schools through their parents or grandparents, they are known as Intergenerational Residential School Survivors. From our survey, the most prevalent losses experienced by intergenerational survivors of the residential school system have been losses of love, family and identity.

51% of the respondents of the residential school questionnaire completed by the intergenerational survivors indicated the lack of affection shown to them by their parents, which has resulted in their inability as adults to connect to their own emotions due to the residential school syndrome within their families. "I was emotionally neglected by my parents and left wanting love and acceptance. My feelings are frozen because of this and I am unable to show my feelings to others." Survivors of the Mohawk Institute learned to distance themselves from their emotions as a survival mechanism in order to endure the physical, mental, emotional and spiritual abuse they experienced and/or were exposed to. The residential school survivors who completed our survey continually noted that the emotional environment of that institution, created by the adult figures in charge of the children, was very cold and distant. There was no informal interaction between the staff and the children. The children were referred to by numbers assigned to them when they were admitted; they walked in rows, stood in lines and were directed through their daily routines with bells and whistles. With little or no contact from family, it is not surprising that after becoming adults and having families of their own, the residential school survivors were not able to be affectionate, loving parents. They grew into adulthood without parenting skills beyond providing a house, food and clothing.

A lack of parenting skills and distant relationships with immediate and extended family members was identified by 40% of the intergenerational survivors. "I have very little contact with other family members. There is no affection in our relationships." This loss of healthy family relationships has a major effect on our community as a whole since family is of fundamental importance in Haudenosaunee culture. Our relationships to each other as well as how we are to treat one another are articulated in the Great Law and the Code of

Handsome Lake, two main doctrines of Haudenosaunee worldview. In all parts of the culture, the family is of utmost importance to the spiritual development of the people.

The Mohawk Institute removed the children from their families as well as from the community. The children lived at the Institute for ten months of the year and some of them lived there for the whole year. This displacement from the home did not allow for the children to learn how to relate to other people, especially in a family setting. In our teachings, we are told that we learn how to be parents from our parents; we learn to be aunties and uncles from our aunties and uncles; we learn to be grandparents from our grandparents; we learn to be partners from watching how our parents care for one another.

Because the survivors of the Institute learned to be individuals, needing to think of themselves for their immediate survival, they were not able to think of others or the future generations. They were not taught our teachings of interconnectedness among the family, clan, and nation which not only gave them a natural system of support, but also taught them their roles and responsibilities to all levels of society. Further, they were not aware of how their choices would affect everyone in that system just as they are affected by the choices made by others.

A loss of identity, including language and culture was recognized by 15% of the intergenerational survivor respondents. "I have experienced a loss of identity, language and culture. My grandfather refused to teach the language to his kids or grandchildren." Our identity is a gift given to us from the Creator. Like all gifts from the Creator we must be thankful and respect who we were created to be. Therefore, to develop a strong identity, we must be allowed to learn the ways and worldview of our people. That is what the Creator has given us to understand ourselves and the world around us. The intention of the residential school was to have children abandon their traditional ways and learn to be like the English-Canadian people with Christian values. Children were forced to attend church and were educated through a Christian value system. They were told that the Haudenosaunee way of life was heathen or savage. They were threatened with stories of hell and condemnation should they not accept the Christian belief system.

The children in the Mohawk Institute were forbidden to speak their languages. The government and others who intended to assimilate the Haudenosaunee saw no need for children to maintain their original languages. As a result, survivors were then reluctant to teach their children the culture and language. Today, a loss of language fluency greatly affects the community of Six Nations since our languages are a major source of validation for our people. All of the ceremonies of the Haudenosaunee are done in one of the five original Haudenosaunee languages. The language of the Haudenosaunee provides a way of seeing the world. Children who are not taught their languages lose that way of understanding their surroundings.

For the Haudenosaunee people, an understanding of the culture is also essential to the development of a positive identity, a strong spirit and healthy connection to all of creation. Within the culture we learn the principles of peace, strength and a good mind. We learn to have a sense of community. We learn songs, dances, ceremonies, and medicines. As well, the duties of a man and a woman in a relationship, as individuals, within the clan, within the nations and within the league of nations, are all articulated in our original teachings.

Many of the intergenerational survivors came into service at **Ganǫhkwásra'** expressing a desire to reclaim the culture, traditions and language of their ancestors. All expressed a need to be released from the generational pain, fear, anger and shame from the Residential Schools era, and a hope to learn how to be in healthy relationships with themselves, their children, others, and with the Creator.

To be fair, it must be noted that this survey did not specifically inquire about positive experiences. However, if there were positive experiences to speak of, there was room to record these experiences when asked questions such as: "What traumas (losses) or experiences were you exposed to within the Residential School?"; and, "How has this experience affected your life?" Many intergenerational respondents did respond that traumas experienced by family members were unknown to them.

At Ganohkwásra⁷, we believe that every community member has been affected by the residential school system since our teachings tell us we are all a part of an interconnected circle of life - what affects one, affects all. It has therefore been a very painful process for our counsellors to hear the specific stories passed on by word of mouth from family members seeking services. And as the years go by, more and more residential school survivors pass away taking secrets and memories of their experiences with them.

The survey that was conducted was our attempt to explore the losses experienced by families within our community. Perhaps we will never truly know the impact these residential school experiences has had, and continues to have, on our community members. To gain a clearer picture of the residential school experiences, all we can do is pay attention when survivors and intergenerational survivors choose to share their truths. Most of all, we need to believe and respect those truths.

What do past experiences at residential school have to do with healing from sexual abuse? Sexual assault healing involves grieving losses. At Ganohkwásra⁷, we acknowledge the need to grieve personal, family and generational losses in a safe and healing way. Some level of self-forgiveness and an ability to accept and let go of personal mistakes is often achieved by program participants as grief is explored. Our teachings tell us that we are all vulnerable to the positive and negative energies in this world and no one is exempt from that. Taking responsibility for self is very empowering and freeing within the healing process.

To date (August 2004), Sonhatsí:wa has worked with 76 program participants as well as a number of others regarding sexual traumas (ie. other program participants, crisis situations etc.), including men, women, youth and children. As an organization we have undertaken an on-going historical case study of the Sonhatsí:wa program participants, documenting and accumulating the specific details of their historical sexual traumas in order to develop statistical data that reveals a high risk sexual assault profile within our community. The hope is that this study will be used as a prevention strategy, allowing community members to learn from our past to ensure the safety and protection of our children today, as well as for the future generations. The statistics presented at this time are based on a random selection of 30 female participants, between the ages of 18 and 62 years. All participants in this case study are First Nations participants, Six Nations community members, residential school survivors and/or intergenerational residential school survivors.

Thus far, this study has revealed the following information which is based on 193 allegations of sexual assault experienced by the 30 female survey participants: 41% occurred when the victims were between the ages of 6-12 years while 28% occurred between the ages of 13-18 years; 55% of these sexual assault disclosures occurred at Six Nations while 23% took place in the nearby town or city which they resided at the time; 62% of these sexual assault disclosures occurred within the victim's own home; the second highest place the participants reported the incident occurred was at their grandparent's home (10%); 18% of the sexual violations occurred when children were left with a babysitter; 13% occurred when the participants were left alone in a room with their abuser (parents/other family members were often in the house, but not in the same room); 56% of the sexual violators were reported to be male between the ages of 19 – 49 years; 56% of the cases identified a family member (25% immediate and 31% extended) as being the perpetrator with 16% of them specifically identified as a cousin; An acquaintance (someone known to the victim, but not well enough to be considered a friend) was identified as the perpetrator in 19% of the sexual assault instances; The most common type of sexual assault was identified as child sexual abuse (when a child ages 16 and under is coerced, manipulated or forced and used for the sexual gratification of an older adolescent or adult. ie. sexual touch, fondling) at 31% and child rape (anal, oral or vaginal sex with a child) was identified at 24%.

Therefore, from this historical case study we learn the high risk profile of sexual assault cases have occurred with children between the ages 6-12 years. These children were sexually assaulted by a male family member who was between the ages of 19-49 years. These sexual assault violations occurred when they were left with a babysitter. The participants of this study reported that 65% of these sexual violations occurred through manipulation, coersion, or misuse of trust, power and control over these victims. This is an important fact as it highlights the grooming phase abusers often engage in to manipulate their victims. We feel it is also important to mention that of the total sexual assault disclosures these participants reported, 10% of the perpetrators were identified as female.

In addressing the sexual traumas experienced by program participants, Sonhatsí:wa implements the many techniques described in this book. We have learned that sexual assault is a spiritual trauma. It is a violation of trust and of the spirit that has devastating effects on a person's being – physically, mentally, spiritually and emotionally. When working with individuals, we attempt to address each of these parts and assist the individual to get back to their true self. We also try to help them to heal their perceptions of themselves in regards to their sexuality which has often been completely distorted by their sexual trauma.

Our original teachings tell us we learn about our sexuality from the time we are babies. Traditionally, all of the teachings we receive throughout our childhood teach us about our sexuality because we are taught who we are as men and women, having respect for ourselves as well as respecting and honouring the opposite sex.

From the first years of our life we are with our mother. Our mother and the other women in our family are our first teachers. From them, little girls learn how to conduct themselves as women. They learn, through observation, about what it means to be a woman. Little boys learn about the nature of women. They learn about their hardships and what comforts them. They learn understanding, compassion and respect for women. The women also model, for both boys and girls, how women are to be treated by the way they allow others to treat them. When a child is around nine years of age the men begin to play a more active role in teaching them. Girls learn from their fathers and uncles about sharing healthy, unconditional love with men. They also learn about different kinds of men. It is the men's responsibility to show the girls the different behaviours of men, the choices men can make for themselves and the lives they have as a result. The boys learn from men about their responsibilities as men. While still quite young boys are given tools to play with that teach them about their roles. For example, they are given weapons to hunt small game and lacrosse sticks to teach them how to care for their wives, as caring for a lacrosse stick requires commitment and attention.

    The time of changing from childhood to adulthood is marked for girls by their first menstruation cycle, for boys by a change in their voices. When these changes begin to happen, the mothers, aunties and grandmothers, fathers, uncles and grandfathers talk to the young people about the changes they are experiencing in their minds, bodies and spirits. They also speak to them about how their lives will change as they become men and women, taking their place within the family and community. The young men and women are warned of the yearning they will have to be sexually active. They say at that time their attraction to each other will be strong because their bodies are getting ready to reproduce. We are told it is very important to keep them apart or to be sure they are properly supervised by parents and extended family during this time. Although their bodies may be telling them they are ready to be sexually active, their mind, heart, and spirit are not. So, we are to encourage them to enjoy their friendships and not to worry about sexual relationships until they are really prepared for the responsibilities and commitment involved.

    At this time the men and women are also to explain to the young people what sex is really about. We were given sex as a means of fulfilling our responsibility to continue human life on the earth. When we choose to have sex it's like we are asking the Creator to bless us with a child. We are telling him we are ready for the responsibilities of supporting and nurturing life.

    Sex is not a physical act separate from the mental, emotional, and spiritual parts of our being. Physically it is when a man and a woman share their bodies with one another totally. Our bodies are sacred. Our bodies are our lodges for our spirits and like all other things in creation - they are gifts from the Creator. We need to care for them and honour them. Therefore, sex is a very special act between two people. We are putting our bodies together to make a connection that is offering a place for a baby's spirit.

There are also emotional attachments that occur when we have sex. Our emotional needs to feel love and acceptance as well as joy, excitement, pleasure and belonging are all met in positive sexual acts. Our love is overflowing in those moments and that is also special. It's important because when we've created a new life, the baby needs to feel love between the parents right from the moment it is conceived. After becoming sexually intimate with someone we have an emotional and spiritual attachment to them. We have shared something very significant and with that comes a lot of feelings, emotions and a deep connection.

Mentally, we also share our minds in positive sexual acts. We give all of our attention to our partner during that time. We need to think of them and respect our partner. How do they feel? Are they comfortable? Are they enjoying themselves? What could you do for them? Our thoughts are very important. Making sure we remember to have good thoughts and thus a good mind adds to a positive experience. Our thoughts also need to be positive, so if a baby should come from that connection they will be learning about a good mind right from the start.

Sex is also very spiritual. Haudenosaunee people say that we were once so spiritually connected that men and women didn't need to have sex to make a baby. They only had to lie with the bottoms of their feet pressed together. Now, we do need sex to have babies and when we do it is a time when our spirits are joined. Our individual powers as a man and a woman to create life are brought together. It is truly spiritual because from that union a door is created for a new spirit to move from the spirit world to the physical world. This is the beginning of new life.

When our children are raised with these teachings, abuse does not happen because the respect for self and others is there. The need for power and control over another is not there because men and women are strong and confident within themselves.

We feel it is important to mention here that although we believe in the learning of our culture and traditions as a way to restore family units, to revitalize our community and nations, and to heal from our traumas, we also recognize the times when violence was a part of our past. We are not blind to the fact that unfortunate incidents of family violence and/or sexual assault may have occurred in our original societies; however, we are confident that our social structures ensured that these incidents were dealt with promptly and justly since living communally, with our extended families, was a powerful form of social control. Traditional people in our community have shared with us the ways in which these types of behaviours were dealt with which ranged from having counsels with Clan and Nation leaders to banishment from the village which consequently would often result in death.

In their healing work from sexual traumas many participants of the **Sonhwatsíwa** program have struggled with forgiveness and acceptance of self. They make choices to change their life for the better yet have a difficult time letting go of the guilt and shame of the past. Again, to find what we need to deal with these issues we can look for in our teachings.

There are many stories that teach us of forgiveness and the ability we have to make positive changes for ourselves. Tekarihoken, one of the first of the Mohawk Chiefs was once a cannibal. Upon seeing the kindness and gentleness of the Peacemaker's face his mind was changed. With the help of the Peacemaker he vowed to change his evil ways and focus his energy on working for the benefit and health of the people. Tsakonhsase, the first woman to accept the message of peace, was once an evil-minded woman. Her house was positioned along a path frequently travelled by men. She would invite them to stop for a rest in her home, make them a nice meal and encourage them to continue their ways by feeding their hatred with gossip. The Peacemaker saw this and with his words of what peace could bring to her, convinced her to change. She then committed herself to using her energy to do good for the people. Another example of change is Atotarho. Atotarho was an evil sorcerer among the Onondaga people. He was so evil he had snakes coming from his hair and his body was grossly disfigured in seven places. He would use his power to manipulate and control the people. When the five nations of people had agreed to come together they united in an effort to stop Atotarho's evil ways. With the help of the Peacemaker the people approached Atotarho. The songs of peace that were sung changed Atotarho's mind and the Peacemaker rubbed down his body, removing the snakes from his hair and straightening out the seven crooks in his body, to show him the strength and beauty he possessed. Atotarho was then recognized as the first Chief of the Onondaga people who were given the responsibility of watching over the central fire of the Haudenosaunee Confederacy.

As a people we have had times when our entire nations strayed from our original teachings. Our people took part in wars, adultery, witchcraft, alcoholism and destructive treatment of each other. It was during those times, the worst times of our history, that we have received our greatest teachings through prophets sent by the Creator. The first time was when we received our Four Sacred Ceremonies, the next when we received the Great Laws of Peace and finally, when we received the Good Message spread through our nations by Handsome Lake.

Today, we can look to our history for teachings that apply to our own experiences and struggles. We can learn to forgive and accept all people. We learn to have confidence in ourselves, that everyone can make positive change for themselves regardless of the past. We are reassured that good things can come from the worst situations. We can let go of the pain and reconnect with our true selves.

At Ganohkwásra' we lean on these teachings to give people hope. It was the original goal of Wilma General, Reva Bomberry and the other founding board members to end family violence in our community. As an organization we have not lost sight of that goal and we will continue to strive for it. We know it is not unrealistic because our history tells us our people have come through the worst of times. We have always learned from our mistakes and wrong doings. The lessons that come from hard times have continually made us stronger and more beautiful.

The Healing Journey of First Nations People

For many of the individuals who have shared their heart and soul within the pages of this book, finding their way back to the original ways of Onkwehon:we (First Nations) people has been the strongest part of their healing. Finding their true selves meant learning who they are as Onkwehon:we people. Our teachings tell us that in order to feel complete we must honour that special part of ourselves - the spirituality that was given to us by the Creator. It brings us back to the basics of life. It helps us to see the world as a simple and peaceful place. It means giving thanks for a new day, acknowledging our connection to all of creation by extending our greetings and love.

To move forward we must first understand ourselves in the present. To understand the present we must understand the past. In doing that we are planting our roots so we are grounded in knowing where we came from as a people, as a family, and as individuals. We can rejoice in the events that call for celebration and grieve the events that have caused feelings of loss and pain. Either way, we go through what is needed and move forward, taking with us the lessons we are given from both positive and negative occurrences of the past. It is only then that we can build a strong identity as we are able to identify behaviours and cycles for what they are. This is the first step to making choices for positive change.

At the time when only First Nations people lived here in North America, our world was full. As a people, we had all we needed to exist. Our societies included governance, education, social organization, means of expression (art), tools and technology, economic structures, ecological preservation, recreation, belief systems, language and clothing. These systems also allowed for the inclusion of love, communication, interconnectedness, purpose, support mechanisms, feelings, medicines, identity, physical attributes, songs, ceremonies, loyalty and leadership. Having such wealth, we had a total sense of purpose and identity in our world, complete with responsibilities to our families, clans, nations and creation. Included in these responsibilities was the responsibility of each individual to uphold and support the safety and continuance of our way of life. Each of us helped in ensuring that our ways were carried with respect so they would be passed on to the future generations.

Throughout time to the present day, First Nations people have experienced many changes to our world. We knew there would be a day when visitors would come from across the ocean. When that time came we shared what we had. Initially, the Europeans needed the First Nations people as partners in the fur trade, allies in war time, and our assistance in learning how to live in a "foreign" wilderness. As time went on the Europeans were able to survive independently in this land that was new to them. They were able to create their own settlements and establish systems of government. Eventually, more and more of them came from across the ocean.

The fur trade, diseases, wars, Indian Act policies, attempts at religious conversion, treaties, and residential schools all played a part in depleting the minds, bodies and spirits of the First Nations people. All of these historical eras or traumas wreaked havoc on our original way of being. Our societal systems were changed drastically as they were not recognized for the elaborate structures they were, but were thought of as non-existent or savage by our one-time friends. Depletion in Onkwehonwe populations, the wars undertaken to eradicate our belief systems and displacements to foreign lands, robbed our people of our original laws and customs that sustained our communities which supported families and individuals. These traumas then left us with a legacy of violence, alcoholism, abuse, neglect, disrespect, foreign belief systems and a weakened leadership.

In Haudenosaunee culture, family is of fundamental importance to our well-being. It is the responsibility of our family to pass on to us the teachings of our ancestors which teach us how to live in balance with the world around us. Traditionally, these family structures include our relations far beyond our immediate, nuclear family. We are a part of a larger, extended family, a clan. Our clan family provides our foundation for life. It is here that we found our sense of identity, our place in society, and where we learned the knowledge and skills needed to support the physical, mental, emotional and spiritual well-being of ourselves and those around us.

However, our original systems have been eroded by imposed systems of power and control; systems that have influenced the way we think and feel about ourselves. This has resulted in generations of family violence and sexual assault causing us to lose our connection to the universe, to Creator's love, and to our true selves. Life has become full of pain; complicated and distorted. Throughout our history we have experienced an insurmountable amount of loss which includes our understanding of our interconnectedness, responsibility, equality, family, and most relevant to the purposes of this book, our understanding and respect for healthy sexuality. These losses have created a great imbalance in the total well-being of our people. It may be difficult to understand how past historical losses and traumas continue to affect the First Nations people of today. One could easily assume it is simply a matter of choice to move on. However, the difficulty in getting past historical trauma increases as these generational traumas are passed down from generation to generation within the very cells of each individual. These "blood-memories" become a part of our current, collective unconscious, that resulting in even further pain experienced by the people of Six Nations and First Nations as a whole.

For generations now, many of our people have experienced childhoods of abuse and neglect. As illustrated in the stories shared in this book, children carry the effects of childhood trauma into their adult lives. Whatever form those effects take, they stifle people from becoming the truly wonderful beings they were created to be. Fortunately, many adults and young people are now looking back to our original way of being to help them with healing from historical and childhood traumas, as well as understanding generational losses. They are learning what should have been given to them as children. They are re-parenting their inner child with the traditional values of our people, allowing them to become adults today with good minds, loving hearts and strong spirits. They are ending the cycle of violence that has been so prevalent in our communities for too long. They are committing themselves to new lives with ancient ways, not only for themselves, but for their children and their grandchildren, and for the unseen faces of seven generations to come. Our people have proven their strength to persevere by the simple fact that we are here. Now, those days are ending when we are merely surviving, for we are beginning to live, we are beginning to thrive. Our culture and our teachings are returning to the hearts and the minds of our people. Today we stand proud as strong Onkwehonwe people and strong Onkwehonwe nations.

Maintaining A Good Mind

Put a cornhusk-braided mat at your door:
Corn is one of our greatest gifts. The husks on the corn are a symbol of guidance and nourishment. As the kernels of corn grow, the husk wraps itself around them. It is there to hold and guide the corn while also keeping out anything that may cause harm. The cornhusk mat can do the same for our homes. As people enter, the cornhusk will help to prevent any negative energy from entering into your home.

Sweep around your doors and your walkway every morning:
Use a broom and sweep your entire doorway. Then, continue to sweep your porch or front step and out along your walkway. While sweeping, ask that if anything had been put in your path to cause you or your family harm, it will be swept away and your path for the day will be clear and safe.

Give thanks:
Give thanks every morning and every night for what we have. Humbling ourselves and taking the time to be grateful can help us to have more peaceful minds.

Open a window to let the negativity out:
The air around us will hold the energy we put into it. Opening a window allows the wind to take any negative energy away. It is the job of the wind to clean the air of negativity.

Go outside:
Let the wind clean your mind. That's part of it's job too. Let it carry away whatever may be bothering you. Let the earth take the negative energy away from your feet. The earth is our mother. She provides us with love and support. She will take our pain away from our heart through our feet. She knows how to care for that energy.

Use water:
Wash your face with cold water in the morning and drink water

regularly. If you are feeling troubled, splash cold water on your face. The crispness of really cold water helps to clean our minds. We use water with children and sometimes we need it to help us as well.

What is Sexual Assault?

Sexual Assault is any unwanted act of a sexual nature imposed by one person upon another. Forced coerced intercourse, grabbing, touching or kissing can be defined as sexual assault.

> ****Sexual Assault is an act of violence, control and domination. It is a criminal offence.****

What Is Consent?

Consent is based on the ability to choose.
Consent is active, not passive.
Consent is only possible through equal power. Giving in, going along to fit in, being deceived,
or being put on a "guilt trip" are examples of manipulation, not consent.

Consensual sex is when two consenting adults have agreed to participate in a sexual activity under their own free will.

Did you know …?

Your partner does not have a right to sex because you are married or in a relationship. You have a choice to consent, or object, to any sexual activity regardless of your relationship with someone.

When a person is intoxicated, they are considered not able to give consent to sexual activity.

Children cannot consent to sexual activity.

Anyone convicted of a sexual assault faces a maximum penalty of 10 years to life imprisonment.

If you have recently been sexually assaulted ...

Go to a safe place.
Call the police if you need protection or want to report the assault.
Seek medical attention from your doctor, a clinic, or the hospital emergency.
Get support from someone you trust.
Do not wash or try to fix yourself up. You may be destroying important evidence that could be used later, if you decide to press charges.
Keep anything that could be used as evidence such as clothes and bedding.
Leave the scene as it is, do not clean or pick things up.

If you were sexually abused as a child ...

Sexual abuse of children is not a new problem, but it is a crime that more people are able to talk about today. And that is a good beginning.

Many survivors of childhood sexual abuse continue, as adults, to experience personal difficulties related to the abuse. Many have benefited from counselling or self-help groups. If you are trying to come to grips with the impacts of a past experience, there are counselling agencies that can assist you.

Survivors of sexual abuse are encouraged to report past incidents of sexual abuse and to identify the alleged offender, especially if he or she has direct contact with children.

If you are a male survivor of sexual assault ...

Remember, men and boys are at equal risk of being sexually assaulted. Sexual assault of males is not uncommon.

It is common for men/boys to experience confusion in regards to their sexuality. Having been sexually assaulted by a same sex perpetrator does not mean that you are homosexual or will become homosexual.

A few reasons why sexual assault of men and boys is unlikely to be reported:
- Society expects boys and men to be more sexual – sexual activity is often assumed to be positive
- Fear of being associated with homosexuality
- Assumption/expectation of males to be able to protect themselves – "Real men can't be raped"
- Society romanticizes men/boys being seduced by women
- Men and boys are socialized not to express their feelings

If you can relate to these situations, remember that any form of unwanted sexual activity is a violation of your spirit. It is okay for men to say "no." You decide who you will share yourself with. When the power to make that decision has been taken from you, through force or coersion, you are experiencing a form of abuse and this is not acceptable.

Flashbacks

Flashbacks are one of the most common experiences that occur when a person begins to remember having been sexually abused. Flashbacks are moments of reliving the trauma, or some part of the trauma, as if it were happening in the present. Flashbacks come in the form of memories (ie. pictures in the mind), sights, sounds, smells, body sensations or numbness. One may also have a sense of panic, being trapped or feeling powerless with no specific memory of the trauma. These experiences can also happen repeatedly within one's dreams.

If you have experienced sexual trauma, you may know very well the sensation of flashbacks and how frightening they can be for an individual. Survivors often become overwhelmed with fear and panic due to flashbacks. Many sexual abuse survivors report feeling overwhelmed and "paralyzed" with fear due to flashbacks occurring during any form of sexual intimacy. This can be very confusing and scary for both the survivor and the survivor's partner. We highly recommend that your partner, who is also affected by the sexual abuse as a secondary victim, get support as well. Many sexual abuse survivors report feeling like they are going "crazy" during these episodes. It is important to know that flashbacks are very normal and will likely occur to anyone who has experienced trauma such as sexual abuse. It is often an indication that the person is feeling safe. The spirit allows these memories to emerge, knowing the person is able, today, to manage these memories, thoughts and feelings. With guidance and support, they will pass.

Below is a list of coping techniques you can do to help yourself if you are experiencing flashbacks:
1. Tell yourself that you are having a flashback, and that it simply means you are healing from the trauma.
2. Breathe in deeply from your nose, feeling the coolness of the air, and blowing the warmth of your breath slowly out through your mouth. When we get scared, we normally stop breathing. As a result, our body starts to panic due to the lack of oxygen. This lack of oxygen in itself causes a great deal of panic-like feelings; pounding in the head, dizziness and

shakiness.
3. Get grounded, focusing your attention on the strength, security and sturdiness of the floor or ground under your feet. Imagine you have sacred roots attached to the bottom of your feet. When you breathe in, imagine you are taking in the energy, love and security of our mother, the earth, from these sacred roots.
4. Re-orient yourself to the present. Begin to use your five senses as soon as you are aware you are having a flashback. Name what you see, hear or smell, either out loud or within your own self. What colours do you see around you? What shapes do you see? Are people nearby? Listen to the sounds in the room; hear yourself taking deep breaths; hear the traffic outside, the birds. Feel yourself in your body; the clothing touching your skin; your chair underneath you. Rub your arms and hands. Identify the smells within the room. Feel the cool air within your nostrils as you breath.
5. Take time to recover. These are very powerful experiences. Honour your experience and the fact that you have survived. Take a nap or a warm bath. Smudge and cleanse yourself with healing medicines such as sage.
6. Seek out someone to talk to (ie. friend, counsellor). If you are not currently seeing a counsellor or therapist, now is a good time to start.

Resources

The following is a short list of possible resources concerning family violence and sexual assault as well as residential schools and Haudenosaunee culture. This list is not exhaustive by any means. If you require more information or assistance please seek out services and resources more specific to your needs or those locally available.

Support

Ganǫhkwásra' Family Assault Support Services
P.O. Box 250, 1781 Chiefswood Rd.
Ohsweken, ON, Canada
N0A 1M0
Ph: 519-445-4324
Fax: 519-445-4825
E-mail: ganohkwa@execulink.com
Website: www.ganohkwasra.com

Assaulted Women's Helpline
1-866-863-0511
TTY 1-866-863-7868

National Aboriginal Circle Against Family Violence
396 Cooper Street, Suite 301
Ottawa, ON
K2P 2H7
Ph: 613-236-1844
Fax: 613-236-8057
Website: www.nacafv.ca

To find a shelter near you check out this website: www.shelternet.ca

Books

Barman, Jean, Yvonne Hebert and Don McCaskill.
    1995 Indian Education in Canada Volume 1: The

Legacy. Vancouver: University of British Columbia Press.

Battiste, Marie, and Jean Barman.
    1995   First Nations Education in Canada: The Circle Unfolds. Vancouver: University of British Columbia Press.

Graham, Elizabeth.
    1996 The Mush Hole: Life at Two Indian Residential Schools. Waterloo, ON: Heffle Publishing.

Jaine, Linda.
    1993 Residential Schools: The Stolen Years. Saskatchewan: University Extensive Press, University of Saskatchewan.

Mitchell, Michael (Kanentakeron), Barbara (Kawenehe) Barnes, eds., et. al.
    1984 Traditional Teachings. Cornwall Island: North American Indian Travelling College.

Parker, A.C..
    1990 The Code of Handsome Lake: The Seneca Prophet. Ohsweken: Iroquois Reprints.

Pettit, Jennifer.
    1993 From the Longhouse to the Schoolhouse: The Mohawk Institute 1834-1970. London: Faculty of Graduate Studies, University of Western Ontario.

Thomas, Jacob.
    1995 Teachings From the Longhouse. Toronto: Stoddart Publishing Co. Ltd.

Shimony, Annemarie Anrod
    1994 Conservatism Among the Six Nations Iroquois. New York: Syracuse University Press.

We Would Love to Hear From You

If you would like to contact our organization to provide feedback or ask questions, we would love to hear from you. You can fill out the feedback form and mail it to the following address:

Ganohkwásra' Family Assault Support Services
P.O. Box 250, 1781 Chiefswood Rd.
Ohsweken, Ontario, Canada
N0A 1H0

Or you can visit our website and complete an on-line form at: www.ganohkwasra.com

Or simply email us at: ganohkwasra@sixnationsns.com

Sonhatsí:wa Feedback Form

What was your initial reaction upon completing this book?

Have the stories within this book had an impact on your life? If so, in what way?

Has reading this book been a learning experience for you? If so, in what way?

Have the stories within this book increased your awareness of child sexual abuse, what to look for and how to prevent it? Additional comments?

Is there a message you would like to send to one (or more) of the participants who contributed their healing story to this book?

If Ganǫhkwásra⁷ were to undertake the publication of another book, what specific focus would you like to see?

Acknowledgements

Writer/Editor - Stacy Tekonwanyahesen Hill
Stacy is from the Turtle Clan (Sha'tekarihwate) of the Mohawk Nation (Kanyenkehaka) at the Six Nations of the Grand River Territory where she resides with her husband and their children. Stacy holds the culture and traditions of Haudenosaunee people close to her heart, believing strongly that these are the integral components of healing and wellness for our people.

Ganohkwasra wishes to acknowledge Stacy Hill, Writer/Editor for giving so much of herself to this project. "Stacy you carry the kindness, wisdom, integrity and spirit of our people. You give us all hope for our future generations to come."

Illustrator - Raymond R. Skye
Born to the Tuscarora Nation, Raymond Skye is a resident of the Six Nations of the Grand River Territory. Raymond has worked diligently to distinguish himself as an artist of talent and ability. Using pastel and watercolour, Raymond enjoys the challenge that art brings him. He readily admits his largest challenge is to find the time to paint as much as he would like to.

Teiethinonweraton (We give our thanks, greetings and love) to the late Wilma General (kenha) and Reva Bomberry for their vision and determination to make **Ganǫhkwásra⁷** a reality for our community. Teiethinonweraton ne Norma General, Dan Longboat, Tom Porter, Germaine Myke, Wendy Thomas, Elva Jamieson, Alfred Keye, Tom Deer, Marjorie Henry and the Haudenosaunee Resource Centre for sharing their strength and wisdom in regards to the history and culture of our people. Teiethinonweraton ne Rick Monture for his patience and proofreading skills. Teiethinonweraton ne **Saho⁷nikonrí:io⁷ne**

(Mens' Program) for the healing work accomplished with the male participants of this book, and for being a trail blazer in working with sexual assault traumas at Ganǫhkwásra'. Teiethinonweraton ne Jean Doolittle, Alice Bomberry, and Liz Williams for their support and guidance. Teiethinonweraton ne Doris Henry (current Director), the Board of Directors and the staff of Ganǫhkwásra' for their commitment and dedication to working towards ending family violence in our community. Teiethinonweraton ne the eleven poetry contributors for adding those special pieces which tell of their own healing journeys. Teiethinonweraton again to the individuals who made this project possible by being so brave as to share a piece of themselves within the pages of this book. Finally, teiethinonweraton ne the Aboriginal Healing Foundation and Canadian Heritage for the funding that made this project possible.

Closing

As we begin, we must end. In all of our gatherings and ceremonies we offer thanks once again to end our doings and to send people off in a good way. It brings our work full circle, to a close. So, within this book, it only feels proper to do the same as we acknowledge the work that has been put into this book; the lives, tears, and teachings shared, have meant so much to the people involved. For a time this has been healing work. For now, this piece is finished so we will bring it to a close with thanksgiving for all that has occurred.

And so, to end we extend our thanks, greetings and love for the people, that everyone is at peace.

We extend our thanks, greetings and love to our Mother, the Earth.

We extend our thanks, greetings and love to the waters on the earth.

We extend our thanks, greetings, and love to the plant life, the vegetables and fruit as well as the medicines and the trees.

We extend our thanks, greetings and love to the free, wild animals and the birds.

We extend our thanks, greetings and love to the four winds and our Grandfathers, the thunders.

We extend our thanks, greetings and love to our Elder Brother, the Sun, our Grandmother, the Moon and the stars in the night time sky.

We extend our thanks, greetings and love to the Four Beings that watch over us from above.

We extend our thanks, greetings and love to the Peacemaker and Handsome Lake for all they have done for us.

We extend our thanks, greetings and love to **Shonkwaya'tihson**, the one who made you.

For now, this is all we can do. And now it is done. Tahnon onen etho